The BEGINNER'S DICTIONARY of Prayerbook Hebrew

Ethelyn Simon

and

Irene Resnikoff

EKS PUBLISHING COMPANY, OAKLAND, CALIFORNIA

Classical Hebrew Educational Materials

Research Editor
Alan K. Lipton

Consultants
Rabbi Neal Scheindlin
Dvora Weisberg

Aramaic Consultant
Pinchas Giller

Book Design
Irene Imfeld

Cover Design
Margareta Bergman-Slutzkin

Typesetting
Ari Davidow/*turnaround*

ISBN 0-939144-13-1

© 1989 by EKS Publishing Company

Second Printing 1992

5346 College Avenue
Oakland, California 94618

P.O. Box 11133
Oakland, California 94611

Table of Contents

וְכָל־בָּנַיִךְ לִמּוּדֵי יְיָ, וְרַב שְׁלוֹם בָּנָיִךְ

Isaiah 54:13

All your children shall be taught of the Lord,
and great shall be the peace of your children.

To all my children, grandchildren, and their children to come.

How To Use This Dictionary

Why Is This Dictionary Different From All Other Hebrew Dictionaries?

Most Hebrew dictionaries list the words alphabetically by their root forms. If you do not know the root, you are unable to locate the word. In this dictionary the words are listed in the same grammatical forms as they appear in the prayerbook. Therefore you do not need to know any Hebrew grammar in order to find the words you want. *The Beginner's Dictionary of Prayerbook Hebrew* was designed specifically to be easy to use.

How Did We Choose These Words?

We actually counted every Hebrew word in *The Daily Prayer Book* (Philip Birnbaum, 1977); *Gates of Prayer* (Central Conference of American Rabbis, 1975); and the center 400 pages of *Mahzor for Rosh Hashanah and Yom Kippur* (The Rabbinical Assembly, 1978). Any word that appeared over 50 times in our count is entered in this dictionary in the form in which it appears in the prayerbook. We then reviewed the most often used prayers in all three of the above books. Any words used in these prayers that were not already in our list were added. We also included common synagogue words and the names of all the festivals.

The Limits of This Dictionary

This dictionary is not meant to be a complete dictionary, or an exhaustive study of prayerbook Hebrew. We have only included those words that are necessary for familiarity with prayer and synagogue vocabulary. However, anyone who knows all the words included in this dictionary will be at home in any Jewish service anywhere.

The Names of God

In accordance with Jewish tradition we are treating the names of God with special respect. In this dictionary they are listed on a separate page and not in the general part of the dictionary.

How Did We Choose These Translations?

In order to find the clearest, most accurate translation, we researched every entry in this dictionary. We consulted dictionaries, concordances, Bibles, and prayerbooks. (See Bibliography.)

To define a word, we first checked for a Biblical reference. Then we consulted several English translations for that reference. We also referred to various prayerbook translations and double checked with Hebrew and English dictionaries. We always chose an English word or phrase that would be easily understood by people of all ages.

How to Translate a Prayer

Good Hebrew is not good English. Therefore a word for word translation will not necessarily sound natural to you. But by actually translating, you can get closer to the meaning of the prayer.

You may need to change the word order. For example, adjectives come after nouns in Hebrew. You may need to add the words **is, am,** or **are** to make sense in English. If a word seems to be missing from the dictionary, remember to look in "The Names of God". Be sure to add the וְ (meaning **and**) when you translate. Compare your translation with an English translation in a prayerbook.

Remember that this is a beginning dictionary, and not *every* word in the prayerbook is listed.

Examples:

loving-kindness	and	grace	blessing	and	goodness	peace	put	← **1**
חֶסֶד	וָ	חֵן	בְּרָכָה	וּ	טוֹבָה	שָׁלוֹם	שִׂים	
your people	Israel	all of	on	and	on us	compassion	and	
עַמֶּךָ	יִשְׂרָאֵל	כָּל	עַל	וְ	עָלֵינוּ	רַחֲמִים	וְ	

before	Moses	put	that	the Torah	is	this	and	← **2**
לִפְנֵי	מֹשֶׁה	שָׂם	אֲשֶׁר	הַתּוֹרָה		זֹאת	וְ	
				Israel		the children of		
				יִשְׂרָאֵל		בְּנֵי		

Aramaic

Although this is a Hebrew dictionary, we have listed the Aramaic of the most popular prayers, including the Kaddish. Aramaic words are shown by the word *(Aramaic).*

Idioms

An idiom, or a group of words peculiar to a language, is shown by the word *(Idiom).* We have also added certain common phrases and called them idioms.

Repeat Listings

Many words in this dictionary are listed more than once. Some words start with the preposition בּ meaning **in** or **with,** the preposition כּ meaning **as,** the preposition ל meaning **to** or **for,** or the preposition מ meaning **from.** These words are listed once independently with the preposition attached, and also sublisted under the word to which they are attached. For example: The word בְּשָׁלוֹם will appear as a main listing in the בּ section, and again as a sublisting under the word שָׁלוֹם. All the words which start with ה meaning **the,** are listed under ה and sublisted under the word to which they are attached. In this way, the dictionary can be used both to find the meanings of prayerbook words and to learn something about how the Hebrew language works.

The Treatment of the ו

The ו meaning **and** is the only prefix that is not given complete repeat listings. According to the instructions at the bottom of the page, we ask the readers to disregard the ו entirely when looking for a word. However, we do give repeat listings to all verbs that start with a reversible ו; that is, a verb which reverses its tense when a ו is attached to it. For example the word וְאָהַבְתָּ meaning **and you shall love,** is listed in the ו section and sublisted under the word אָהַבְתָּ meaning **you have loved.** Other than these verbs, no other words are listed with the ו prefix.

The Dagesh

We have entered every word in the dictionary as if it stands alone, and we have continually followed the classical rules for the dagesh (the dot in the center of the letters). However, in the prayerbook many words appear with a ו prefix and therefore without a dagesh. To avoid confusion, we ask the reader to disregard the dagesh.

Reading Hebrew

For those of you who need a little help reading Hebrew we have included three reading aids. First, at the beginning of the dictionary is a complete Hebrew alphabet chart, which shows you the letters and vowels, and tells you how to pronounce them. Second, at the top of each page you will find a Hebrew alphabet to help you with word order. Third, at the end of the book is a pronunciation guide which lists each word and its pronunciation in English letters.

If you cannot read Hebrew at all, one easy way to learn is by using *Teach Yourself to Read Hebrew,* also published by EKS.

For the Classroom

Here are some ideas for using this dictionary to teach either adults or children in a classroom situation.

I. Translating Prayers
   - A. Give students a Hebrew prayer *without* English translation. Have students use the dictionary to translate the prayer. Be sure to remind them to add **is** and **are,** and to use the "Names of God" section.
   - B. Let students compare their translations with the prayerbook. Use more than one prayerbook if available.

II. Learning About Prefixes in Hebrew
   - A. Have students look up שָׁלוֹם.
     1. Ask students to translate the following words into Hebrew: with peace, the peace, for peace.
     2. Ask students to define לְ, הַ, בְּ, בַּ.
     3. Have students find words with their prefixes listed alphabetically.
   - B. Have students find other examples of words with prefixes.

There are many other ways to teach Hebrew with this dictionary. Even the cover can be used as a teaching tool. We encourage you to be creative. We may publish a teacher's guide at a future date, and we would be interested in hearing about your teaching experiences with this book.

Alphabet Chart

Vowels

Xָ Xַ
a as in y**a**cht

Xִ Xִי
ee as in b**ee**

Xֵ Xֵי
ay as in h**ay**

Xֶ
e as in b**e**d

Xֹ Xוֹ
o as in l**o**w

Xֻ Xוּ
oo as in z**oo**

Xַי
ai as in **ai**sle

Xוֹי
oi as in b**oi**l

Xְ
silent

Consonants

	Book Print	Block	Script	
Silent letter	א	א	א	1
B as in **B**oy **V** as in **V**ine	בּ ב	בּ ב	בּ ב	2
G as in **G**irl	ג	ג	ג	3
D as in **D**oor	ד	ד	ד	4
H as in **H**ouse	ה	ה	ה	5
V as in **V**ine	ו	ו	ו	6
Z as in **Z**ebra	ז	ז	ז	7
CH as in Ba**CH**	ח	ח	ח	8
T as in **T**all	ט	ט	ט	9
Y as in **Y**es	י	י	י	10
K as in **K**itty **CH** as in Ba**CH**	כּ כ ך	כּ כ ך	כּ כ ך	20
L as in **L**ook	ל	ל	ל	30
M as in **M**other	מ ם	מ ם	מ ם	40
N as in **N**ow	נ ן	נ ן	נ ן	50
S as in **S**un	ס	ס	ס	60
Silent letter	ע	ע	ע	70
P as in **P**eople **F** as in **F**ood	פּ פ ף	פּ פ ף	פּ פ ף	80
TS as in Nu**TS**	צ ץ	צ ץ	צ ץ	90
K as in **K**itty	ק	ק	ק	100
R as in **R**obin	ר	ר	ר	200
SH as in **SH**ape **S** as in **S**un	שׁ שׂ	שׁ שׂ	שׁ שׂ	300
T as in **T**all	ת	ת	ת	400

א ב ג ד ה ו ז ח ט י כ ל מ נ ס ע פ צ ק ר ש ת

א

father, the father of	אָב, אַב
the father	הָאָב
as a father	כְּאָב
fathers, ancestors	אָבוֹת, אָבֹת
our fathers, our ancestors	אֲבוֹתֵינוּ, אֲבֹתֵינוּ
to our fathers, ancestors, for our fathers, ancestors	לַאֲבוֹתֵינוּ
our father	אָבִינוּ
Abraham	אַבְרָהָם
to Abraham	לְאַבְרָהָם
master	אָדוֹן
the master of	אֲדוֹן
to the master of	לַאֲדוֹן
powerful, majestic	אַדִּיר
our majestic one, our powerful one	אַדִּירֵנוּ
man	אָדָם
in man	בָּאָדָם
the man	הָאָדָם
as man	כְּאָדָם
to man	לְאָדָם
from man	מֵאָדָם

ground, earth	אֲדָמָה
the ground, the earth	הָאֲדָמָה
love	אַהֲבָה
with love	בְּאַהֲבָה
the love	הָאַהֲבָה
that love which	שֶׁאַהֲבָה
you loved	אָהַבְתָּ
may you love, you shall love	וְאָהַבְתָּ
that you have loved	שֶׁאָהַבְתָּ
the love of	אַהֲבַת
eat	אוֹכְלִין
say, (one) who says	אוֹמֵר, אֹמֵר
the one who says	הָאוֹמֵר
(they) say	אוֹמְרִים
light, the light of	אוֹר
in the light of	בְּאוֹר
as the light of	כְּאוֹר
sign, mark, the sign of	אוֹת
as a sign, as the sign of	לְאוֹת
him, it	אוֹתוֹ, אֹתוֹ
us	אוֹתָנוּ

To find a word:

- Disregard וְ, וּ, וַ, וָ, וֶ or וִ, (meaning **and**) at the beginning of a word.
- Disregard the dot in the center of letters.
- Check "The Names of God" which are listed separately beginning on page 75.
- Insert **am, is, are** wherever needed to make sense of a sentence in English.

א ב ג ד ה ו ז ח ט י כ ל מ נ ס ע פ צ ק ר ש ת

then, at that time . . . . אָז
- from that time . . . . מֵאָז

then . . . . אֲזַי

one, one of, single . . . . אֶחָד, אַחַד
- on the first of . . . . בְּאֶחָד
- the one . . . . הָאֶחָד
- as one of, as one . . . . כְּאֶחָד

after . . . . אַחֲרֵי

one . . . . אַחַת, אֶחָת

where . . . . אַיֵּה

there is no, not, none . . . . אֵין
- without . . . . לְאֵין
- for want of . . . . מֵאֵין
- who is without . . . . שֶׁאֵין

I will fear . . . . אִירָא

man, a man of, the man of . . . . אִישׁ
- the man . . . . הָאִישׁ
- as a man, like a man, as a man of . כְּאִישׁ
- as a man, to a man, for a man of . לְאִישׁ
- from man, from men of . . . . מֵאִישׁ

I will sleep . . . . אִישַׁן

do not . . . . אַל

to . . . . אֶל

only, except . . . . אֶלָּא

these . . . . אֵלֶּה
- in these, with these . . . . בְּאֵלֶּה
- these . . . . הָאֵלֶּה
- like these . . . . כָּאֵלֶּה
- to these . . . . לָאֵלֶּה

to you . . . . אֵלֶיךָ

false gods . . . . אֱלִילִים

if . . . . אִם
- that if . . . . שֶׁאִם

faithfulness . . . . אֱמוּנָה
- with faithfulness . . . . בֶּאֱמוּנָה

his faithfulness . . . . אֱמוּנָתוֹ
- in his faithfulness, for his faithfulness . . . . בֶּאֱמוּנָתוֹ

your faithfulness . . . . אֱמוּנָתְךָ

Amen, so be it . . . . אָמֵן

(he) said . . . . אָמַר
- who said . . . . שֶׁאָמַר

say, (one) who says . . . . . . אֹמֵר, אוֹמֵר

(they) said . . . . אָמְרוּ

To find a word:
- Disregard וְ, וּ, וַ, וָ, וֶ or וִ, (meaning **and**) at the beginning of a word.
- Disregard the dot in the center of letters.
- Check "The Names of God" which are listed separately beginning on page 75.
- Insert **am, is, are** wherever needed to make sense of a sentence in English.

א ב ג ד ה ו ז ח ט י כ ל מ נ ס ע פ צ ק ר ש ת

אִמְרוּ — Say!

אִמְרֵי — the words of
- בְּאִמְרֵי — by the words of

אֱמֶת — truth
- בֶּאֱמֶת — in truth, truly
- הָאֱמֶת — the truth

אָנוּ — we

אֲנַחְנוּ — we
- שֶׁאֲנַחְנוּ — that we

אֲנִי, אָנִי — I
- כְּשֶׁאֲנִי — when I
- שֶׁאֲנִי — that I

אָנֹכִי — I

אֲסוּרִים — bound, imprisoned, the imprisoned ones
- הָאֲסוּרִים — the imprisoned ones

אָעִירָה — I will awake

אַף — anger
- בְּאַף — in anger
- חָרָה אַף — becomes angry, will become angry *(Idiom)*

אֲפִילוּ — even

אֶפֶס — none

אַפְקִיד — I will entrust

אֶקְרָא — I will call

אֲרוֹן הַקֹּדֶשׁ — the holy ark that holds the Torah *(Idiom)*

אֶרֶץ, אָרֶץ — land, the land of, earth
- בָּאָרֶץ — in the land, on earth
- בְּאֶרֶץ — in a land, in the land of
- הָאָרֶץ — the land, the earth
- לָאָרֶץ — to the land, for the land
- מֵאֶרֶץ — from the land of

אֵשׁ — fire, the fire of
- בָּאֵשׁ — with fire
- הָאֵשׁ — the fire
- כָּאֵשׁ — like a fire
- מֵאֵשׁ — from fire, by fire

אֲשֶׁר — who, which, that
- בַּאֲשֶׁר — where, wherever, on account of
- לַאֲשֶׁר — to that which, to wherever
- מֵאֲשֶׁר — from which, from where

אַשְׁרֵי — happy are, happy is

אֶת, אֵת — not translatable (precedes direct object of the sentence)

אַתָּה — you
- כְּשֶׁאַתָּה — when you

To find a word:
- Disregard וְ, וּ, וַ, וָ, וֶ or וִ, (meaning **and**) at the beginning of a word.
- Disregard the dot in the center of letters.
- Check "The Names of God" which are listed separately beginning on page 75.
- Insert **am, is, are** wherever needed to make sense of a sentence in English.

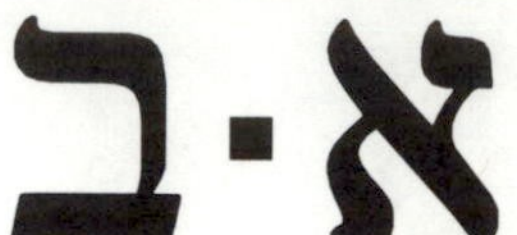

א ב ג ד ה ו ז ח ט י כ ל מ נ ס ע פ צ ק ר ש ת

him, it . . . . אֹתוֹ, אוֹתוֹ

you . . . . אֶתְכֶם

etrog, citron used in . . . . אֶתְרוֹג
celebration of Succot (סֻכּוֹת)

ב

in, at, on, with, ... בְּ, בַּ, בָּ, בֶּ, בִּ
(always attached to the beginning of a word)

(he) comes, (he) came . . . . בָּא

the coming one, next . . . . הַבָּא

that comes . . . . שֶׁבָּא

in man . . . . בָּאָדָם

with love . . . . בְּאַהֲבָה

in the light of . . . . בְּאוֹר

on the first of . . . . בְּאֶחָד

in these, with these . . . . בְּאֵלֶּה

with faithfulness . . . . בֶּאֱמוּנָה

in his faithfulness, ... בֶּאֱמוּנָתוֹ
for his faithfulness

by the words of . . . . בְּאִמְרֵי

in truth, truly . . . . בֶּאֱמֶת

in anger . . . . בְּאַף

in the land, on earth . . . . בָּאָרֶץ

in a land, in the land of . . . . בְּאֶרֶץ

with fire . . . . בָּאֵשׁ

where, wherever, on account of . . . בַּאֲשֶׁר

in the house of . . . . בְּבֵית

in your house . . . . בְּבֵיתְךָ, בְּבֵיתֶךָ

with the son of . . . . בְּבֶן

with the children of, ... בִּבְנֵי
among the children of

with your children . . . . בְּבָנֶיךָ

with the master of . . . . בְּבַעַל

in the morning . . . . בַּבֹּקֶר

in the heights of . . . . בְּגָבְהֵי

with the mighty deeds of . . . . . בִּגְבוּרוֹת

among the nations . . . . בַּגּוֹיִם

by the word . . . . בַּדָּבָר

by the word of . . . . בִּדְבַר

To find a word:

- Disregard וְ, וּ, וַ, וָ, וֶ or וִ, (meaning **and**) at the beginning of a word.
- Disregard the dot in the center of letters.
- Check "The Names of God" which are listed separately beginning on page 75.
- Insert **am, is, are** wherever needed to make sense of a sentence in English.

א ב ג ד ה ו ז ח ט י כ ל מ נ ס ע פ צ ק ר ש ת

in a time	בִּזְמַן
on the holiday of	בְּחַג
in the month	בַּחֹדֶשׁ
in the month of	בְּחֹדֶשׁ
in the lives of (*Aramaic*)	בְּחַיֵּי
in your lifetimes (*Aramaic*)	בְּחַיֵּיכוֹן
life, in life	בַּחַיִּים
with tenderness	בְּחֶמְלָה
with grace, with favor	בְּחֵן
with loving-kindness	בְּחֶסֶד
in your loving-kindness, with your loving-kindness	בְּחַסְדְּךָ, בְּחַסְדֶּךָ
in his desire	בְּחֶפְצוֹ
(he) has chosen	בָּחַר
you have chosen	בָּחַרְתָּ
in the darkness	בַּחֹשֶׁךְ
in goodness	בַּטּוֹב
in your goodness	בְּטוּבְךָ, בְּטוּבֶךָ
before	בְּטֶרֶם

in the words of	בְּדִבְרֵי
in generation after generation, in every generation (*Idiom*)	בְּדוֹר וָדוֹר
with knowledge	בְּדַעַת
on the road	בַּדֶּרֶךְ
on a road, on the road of	בְּדֶרֶךְ
in it, it	בָּהּ
them, in them	בָּהֶם
on the mountain of	בְּהַר
in the mountains	בֶּהָרִים
in it, in him	בּוֹ
your coming	בּוֹאֲכֶם
come in peace (*Idiom*)	בּוֹאֲכֶם לְשָׁלוֹם
create, (one) who creates	בּוֹרֵא
the one who creates	הַבּוֹרֵא
that the one who creates	שֶׁהַבּוֹרֵא
with this	בְּזֹאת
with this	בָּזֶה
in the season	בַּזְּמַן
at this season (*Idiom*)	בַּזְּמַן הַזֶּה

To find a word:

- Disregard וְ, וּ, וַ, וָ, וֶ or וִ, (meaning **and**) at the beginning of a word.
- Disregard the dot in the center of letters.
- Check "The Names of God" which are listed separately beginning on page 75.
- Insert **am, is, are** wherever needed to make sense of a sentence in English.

in me, me . . . . בִּי

with a hand . . . . בְּיָד

through the hand of . . . . בְּיַד

in his hand . . . . בְּיָדוֹ

in the hands of . . . . בִּידֵי

in your hand, in your hands . . בְּיָדְךָ, בְּיָדֵךְ

on the day . . . . בַּיּוֹם

on the day of . . . . בְּיוֹם

on that day *(Idiom)* . . . . . . בַּיּוֹם הַהוּא

in your days . . . . . . *(Aramaic)* בְּיוֹמֵיכוֹן

in the sea . . . . בַּיָּם

bima, pulpit . . . . בִּימָה

in the days of . . . . בִּימֵי

in the days . . . . בַּיָּמִים

in those days *(Idiom)* . . . . . בַּיָּמִים הָהֵם

in our days . . . . בְּיָמֵינוּ

with your right hand . . בִּימִינְךָ, בִּימִינֵךְ

between, among . . . . בֵּין
- from between, from among . . . . . מִבֵּין
- that is between . . . . שֶׁבֵּין

between me . . . . בֵּינִי

with Jacob . . . . בְּיַעֲקֹב

with awe . . . . בְּיִרְאָה

in Jerusalem . . . . בִּירוּשָׁלַיִם

with deliverance . . . . בִּישׁוּעָה

in your deliverance . . . . . . בִּישׁוּעָתְךָ, בִּישׁוּעָתֵךְ

in Israel . . . . בְּיִשְׂרָאֵל

the house of . . . . בֵּית
- in the house of . . . . בְּבֵית
- to the house of . . . . לְבֵית
- from the house of . . . . מִבֵּית

your house, your household . בֵּיתְךָ, בֵּיתֵךְ
- in your house . . . . . בְּבֵיתְךָ, בְּבֵיתֵךְ
- to your house, for your household . . . . . לְבֵיתְךָ, לְבֵיתֵךְ

in glory, in honor . . . . בְּכָבוֹד

in his glory . . . . בִּכְבוֹדוֹ

in your glory . . . . בִּכְבוֹדֵךְ

To find a word:
- Disregard וְ, וּ, וַ, וָ, וֶ or וִ, (meaning **and**) at the beginning of a word.
- Disregard the dot in the center of letters.
- Check "The Names of God" which are listed separately beginning on page 75.
- Insert **am, is, are** wherever needed to make sense of a sentence in English.

ב

א ב ג ד ה ו ז ח ט י כ ל מ נ ס ע פ צ ק ר ש ת

בַּכֹּל	with all, over all
בְּכָל	in all of, with all of, every
בְּכֵן	thus
בְּלֹא	without
בְּלֵב	in the heart of
בְּלֵבָב	with a heart
בְּלִבִּי	in my heart
בְּלִבֵּנוּ	in our hearts
בְּלִי	without
בַּלַּיְלָה	at night
בְּלֶכְתְּךָ	when you are going
בָּם	in them, them
בַּמָּה	How?
בִּמְהֵרָה	quickly
בַּמַּיִם	in the water
בְּמַיִם	in water
בְּמַלְכוּת	in the kingdom of
בְּמַלְכוּתֵהּ	in his kingdom (*Aramaic*)
בְּמַלְכוּתְךָ, בְּמַלְכוּתֶךָ	in your kingdom
בְּמַעֲשֵׂה	with the doing of, with the work of
בְּמַעֲשֶׂיךָ	in your works
בְּמִצְוֹתָיו	with his commandments, in his commandments
בְּמִצְוֹתֶיךָ	in your commandments
בְּמִצְרַיִם	in Egypt
בַּמָּקוֹם	in the place
בְּמָקוֹם	in a place
בִּמְקוֹם	in the place of
בַּמָּרוֹם	on high
בִּמְרוֹמָיו	in his high places
בְּמֹשֶׁה	with Moses
בַּמִּשְׁפָּט	in judgement, justice
בְּמִשְׁפָּט	in judgement, justice
בֵּן	son
הַבֵּן	the son
בֶּן	the son of
בְּבֶן	with the son of
לְבֶן	to the son, to the son of

To find a word:

- Disregard וְ, וּ, וַ, וָ, וֶ or וִ, (meaning **and**) at the beginning of a word.
- Disregard the dot in the center of letters.
- Check "The Names of God" which are listed separately beginning on page 75.
- Insert **am, is, are** wherever needed to make sense of a sentence in English.

ב

א ב ג ד ה ו ז ח ט י כ ל מ נ ס ע פ צ ק ר ש ת

in us, with us, us . . . . בָּנוּ

the sons of, the children of . . . . בְּנֵי

- with the children of, among the children of . . . . בִּבְנֵי
- as the children of . . . . כִּבְנֵי
- to the children of . . . . לִבְנֵי
- from among the children of . . . . מִבְּנֵי

their sons, their children . . . . בְּנֵיהֶם

- to their children, for their children . לִבְנֵיהֶם

his sons, his children . . . . בָּנָיו

your sons, your children . . . . בָּנֶיךָ

- with your children . . . . בְּבָנֶיךָ
- to your children . . . . לְבָנֶיךָ

in the book . . . . בַּסֵּפֶר

in the book of . . . . בְּסֵפֶר

soon . . . . (Aramaic) *בַּעֲגָלָא*

in eternity, in the world . . . . בָּעוֹלָם

with strength, with the strength of . . . . בְּעוֹז

with the help of . . . . בְּעֶזְרַת

in the eyes of . . . . בְּעֵינֵי

in your eyes . . . . בְּעֵינֶיךָ

in our eyes . . . . בְּעֵינֵינוּ

in the city . . . . בָּעִיר

in a city, in the city of . . . . בְּעִיר

the master of, the owner of . . . . בַּעַל

- with the master of . . . . בְּבַעַל

in the world . . . . (*Aramaic*) בְּעָלְמָא

among the people, against the people, the people . . בָּעָם

with a people . . . . בְּעַם

in his people, with his people . . . . . . בְּעַמּוֹ

among the peoples . . . . בָּעַמִּים

with your people, on your people . . . . . . בְּעַמְּךָ, בְּעַמֶּךָ

in the dust . . . . בֶּעָפָר

in the evening . . . . בָּעֶרֶב

on the evening of . . . . בְּעֶרֶב

in the season, in the time . . . . בָּעֵת

at the time of, in the season of . . . . . בְּעֵת

in my mouth, in the mouth of . . . . בְּפִי

in the face of, in front of . . . . בִּפְנֵי

To find a word:

- Disregard וְ, וּ, וַ, וָ, וֶ or וֵ, (meaning **and**) at the beginning of a word.
- Disregard the dot in the center of letters.
- Check "The Names of God" which are listed separately beginning on page 75.
- Insert **am, is, are** wherever needed to make sense of a sentence in English.

א ב ג ד ה ו ז ח ט י כ ל מ נ ס ע פ צ ק ר ש ת

בְּרֵאשִׁית . . . . . in the beginning, creation

בְּרוּחַ . . . . by the spirit of, by the breath of

בָּרוּךְ . . . . blessed, praised

בְּרַחֲמָיו . . . . with his compassion

בְּרַחֲמֶיךָ . . . . with your compassion

בְּרַחֲמִים . . . . with compassion

בְּרִיךְ (Aramaic) . . . . blessed, praised

בְּרִית . . covenant, pledge, binding agreement
- הַבְּרִית . . . . the covenant, the pledge
- לַבְּרִית . for the covenant, for the pledge
- לִבְרִית . . . . for the covenant of, for the pledge of

בֶּרֶךְ . . . . knee

בְּרָכָה . . . . a blessing, blessing
- הַבְּרָכָה . . . . the blessing
- לִבְרָכָה . . . . for a blessing

בָּרְכוּ . . . . Bless! Praise!

בָּרְכוּנִי . . . . bless me

בָּרְכֵנוּ . . . . bless us

בִּרְכָתָא (Aramaic) . . . . blessings

בְּרִנָּה . . . . with joy, with joyous song

בְּצֶדֶק . . . . with righteousness

בִּצְדָקָה . . . . with righteousness

בְּצִיּוֹן . . . . in Zion

בַּצָּרָה . . . . in trouble, in distress

בְּצָרָה . . . . in trouble, in distress

בַּקֹּדֶשׁ . . . . . in holiness, in the holy place

בְּקָדְשׁוֹ . . . in his holiness, in his holy place

בְּקוֹל . . . . . with a voice, with the voice of

בְּקוּמֶךָ . . . . when you are rising up

בֹּקֶר . . . . morning
- בַּבֹּקֶר . . . . in the morning
- הַבֹּקֶר . . . . the morning
- לַבֹּקֶר . . . . in the morning

בְּקָרוֹב . . . . soon

בַּר מִצְוָה . . . . . . Bar Mitzvah, a religious ceremony in which a boy reads the Torah blessings for the first time in front of a Minyan (מִנְיָן)

בָּרָא . . . . (he) created

בְּרָא (Aramaic) . . . . (he) created

בְּרֹאשׁ הַשָּׁנָה . . . . . . on Rosh Hashanah

To find a word:
- Disregard וְ, וּ, וַ, וָ, וֶ or וִ, (meaning **and**) at the beginning of a word.
- Disregard the dot in the center of letters.
- Check "The Names of God" which are listed separately beginning on page 75.
- Insert **am, is, are** wherever needed to make sense of a sentence in English.

א ב ג ד ה ו ז ח ט י כ ל מ נ ס ע פ צ ק ר ש ת

with favor	בְּרָצוֹן
according to your will	בִּרְצוֹנְךָ, בִּרְצוֹנֶךָ
on the seventh	בַּשְּׁבִיעִי
on the Sabbath	בַּשַּׁבָּת
when you are sitting	בְּשִׁבְתְּךָ
with song	בְּשִׁיר
when you are lying down	בְּשָׁכְבְּךָ
with peace	בַּשָּׁלוֹם
with peace	בְּשָׁלוֹם
with your (God's) peace	בִּשְׁלוֹמֶךָ
in the name of, by name	בְּשֵׁם
in his name	בִּשְׁמוֹ
in the heavens	בִּשְׁמֵי
in heaven *(Aramaic)*	בִּשְׁמַיָּא
in the heavens	בַּשָּׁמַיִם
in your name	בִּשְׁמְךָ, בִּשְׁמֶךָ
in the year	בַּשָּׁנָה
on your gates	בִּשְׁעָרֶיךָ

with joy, with delight	בְּשִׂמְחָה
flesh	בָּשָׂר
as flesh	לְבָשָׂר
the flesh of	בְּשַׂר
with joy	בְּשָׂשׂוֹן
daughter, the daughter of	בַּת
Bat Mitzvah, a religious ceremony in which a girl reads the Torah blessings for the first time in front of a Minyan (מִנְיָן) or otherwise demonstrates her Judaic competence in public	בַּת מִצְוָה
in the world	בְּתֵבֵל
with praise	בִּתְהִלָּה
in your praise	בִּתְהִלָּתֶךָ
within us	בְּתוֹכֵנוּ
in the Torah	בַּתּוֹרָה
in the Torah of, in the law of	בְּתוֹרַת
in his Torah	בְּתוֹרָתוֹ
in your Torah	בְּתוֹרָתְךָ, בְּתוֹרָתֶךָ
in glory	בְּתִפְאָרָה
with glory, with the glory of	בְּתִפְאֶרֶת

To find a word:

- Disregard וְ, וּ, וַ, וָ, וֶ or וֵ, (meaning **and**) at the beginning of a word.
- Disregard the dot in the center of letters.
- Check "The Names of God" which are listed separately beginning on page 75.
- Insert **am, is, are** wherever needed to make sense of a sentence in English.

ג

גְּאוּלִים . . . . the redeemed ones, the ones who were saved

גָּאַל . . . . . (the one who) redeemed, saved

גְּאֻלָּה . . . . redemption

גֹּאֲלִי . my redeemer, the one who saves me

גֹּאֲלֵנוּ . our redeemer, the one who saves us

גִּבֹּר, גִּבּוֹר . . . . strong, mighty one

- הַגִּבּוֹר . . . . the strong one
- כְּגִבּוֹר . . . . . . as strong, as strong as

גִּבּוֹר חַיִל . . . mighty man of valor *(Idiom)*

גְּבוּרוֹת, גְּבוּרֹת . . . . . . mighty deeds

- בִּגְבוּרוֹת . . . with the mighty deeds of
- הַגְּבוּרוֹת . . . . the mighty deeds

גָּדוֹל, גָּדֹל . . . . great

- הַגָּדוֹל . . . . the great one

גְּדֻלָּה . . . . greatness

גָּדְלְךָ . . . . your greatness

גּוֹאֵל, גֹּאֵל . . . . . save, (one) who saves, redeem, (one) who redeems

- הַגֹּאֵל . the redeemer, the one who saves

גּוֹאֲלִי, גֹּאֲלִי . . . . my redeemer, the one who saves me

גּוֹי . . . . nation

- הַגּוֹי . . . . the nation
- מִגּוֹי . . . . from a nation

גּוֹיִם . . . . nations

- בַּגּוֹיִם . . . . among the nations
- הַגּוֹיִם . . . . the nations
- לַגּוֹיִם . . . . to the nations

גְּוִיָּתִי . . . . my body

גּוֹמֵל . . . . . (one) who does (usually good)

- הַגּוֹמֵל . the one who does (usually good)

גִּלּוּלִים . . . . idols

גַּם . . . . also

גּוֹרָלֵנוּ . . . . our fate

ד

דַּאֲמִירָן *(Aramaic)* . . . . that we say

דָּבָר . . . . a word, a thing

- בַּדָּבָר . . . . by the word
- הַדָּבָר . . . . the word, the thing
- כַּדָּבָר . . . . according to the word

To find a word:

- Disregard וְ, וּ, וַ, וָ, וֶ or וִ, (meaning **and**) at the beginning of a word.
- Disregard the dot in the center of letters.
- Check "The Names of God" which are listed separately beginning on page 75.
- Insert **am, is, are** wherever needed to make sense of a sentence in English.

ד-ה

א ב ג ד ה ו ז ח ט י כ ל מ נ ס ע פ צ ק ר ש ת

that . . . . *(Aramaic)* דִּי

of all . . . . *(Aramaic)* דְּכָל

Know! . . . . דַּע

knowledge, knowledge of . . . . דַּעַת, דָּעַת
- with knowledge . . . . בְּדַעַת
- the knowledge . . . . הַדַּעַת

of the holy one *(Aramaic)* דְּקֻדְשָׁא, דְּקוּדְשָׁא

generation . . . . דֹּר, דּוֹר

road, road of, way, way of . . . . דֶּרֶךְ
- on the road, on the way . . . . . . בַּדֶּרֶךְ
- on a road, on the road of . . . . . בְּדֶרֶךְ
- the road, the way . . . . הַדֶּרֶךְ

the ways of . . . . דַּרְכֵי

her ways, its ways . . . . דְּרָכֶיהָ

ה

the . . . . הַ, הָ, הֶ
(always attached to the beginning of a word)

indicates a question . . . . הֲ, הַ, הֶ
(always attached to the beginning of a word)

sickness . . . . דֶּבֶר

the word of . . . . דְּבַר
- by the word of . . . . בִּדְבַר
- according to the word of . . . . . כִּדְבַר

the words of . . . . דִּבְרֵי
- in the words of . . . . בְּדִבְרֵי
- from the words of . . . . מִדִּבְרֵי

words, things . . . . דְּבָרִים
- the words, the things . . . . . . הַדְּבָרִים

you spoke . . . . דִּבַּרְתָּ
- may you speak, you shall speak . . . . וְדִבַּרְתָּ

David . . . . דָּוִד, דָּוִיד
- of David . . . . לְדָוִד
- a psalm of David *(Idiom)* . מִזְמוֹר לְדָוִד

my beloved . . . . דּוֹדִי
- to my beloved, for my beloved . . לְדוֹדִי
- come my beloved *(Idiom)* . . . לְכָה דוֹדִי

be like, resembles . . . . דּוֹמֶה

generation . . . . דּוֹר, דֹּר
- in generation after generation, in every generation *(Idiom)* . . . . . . בְּדוֹר וָדוֹר
- from generation to generation, for all generations *(Idiom)* . . . . . . לְדוֹר וָדוֹר

To find a word:
- Disregard וְ, וּ, וַ, וָ, וֶ or וֵ, (meaning **and**) at the beginning of a word.
- Disregard the dot in the center of letters.
- Check "The Names of God" which are listed separately beginning on page 75.
- Insert **am, is, are** wherever needed to make sense of a sentence in English.

א ב ג ד ה ו ז ח ט י כ ל מ נ ס ע פ צ ק ר ש ת

the father	הָאָב
the man	הָאָדָם
the ground, the earth	הָאֲדָמָה
the love	הָאַהֲבָה
the one who says	הָאוֹמֵר
the one	הָאֶחָד
the man	הָאִישׁ
these	הָאֵלֶּה
the truth	הָאֱמֶת
the imprisoned ones	הָאֲסוּרִים
the land, the earth	הָאָרֶץ
the lands	הָאֲרָצוֹת
the fire	הָאֵשׁ
the coming one, next	הַבָּא
Give!	הָבוּ
the one who creates	הַבּוֹרֵא
the son	הַבֵּן
the morning	הַבֹּקֶר
the covenant, the pledge	הַבְּרִית
the blessing	הַבְּרָכָה
the redeemer, the one who saves	הַגֹּאֵל
the strong one	הַגִּבּוֹר
the strength	הַגְּבוּרָה
the mighty deeds	הַגְּבוּרוֹת
Hagaddah, the book used in the celebration of the Passover Seder (סֵדֶר)	הַגָּדָה
the great one	הַגָּדוֹל
the greatness	הַגְּדֻלָּה
the nation	הַגּוֹי
the nations	הַגּוֹיִם
the one who does (usually good)	הַגּוֹמֵל
the meditation of	הֶגְיוֹן
brought us	הִגִּיעָנוּ
the vine	הַגָּפֶן
the word, the thing	הַדָּבָר
the words, the things	הַדְּבָרִים
thanking, praising	הדוֹת, הוֹדוֹת

To find a word:

- Disregard וְ, וּ, וַ, וָ, וֶ or וֵ, (meaning **and**) at the beginning of a word.
- Disregard the dot in the center of letters.
- Check "The Names of God" which are listed separately beginning on page 75.
- Insert **am, is, are** wherever needed to make sense of a sentence in English.

א ב ג ד ה ו ז ח ט י כ ל מ נ ס ע פ צ ק ר ש ת

the knowledge	הַדַּעַת
the road, the way	הַדֶּרֶךְ
that	הַהוּא
on that day *(Idiom)*	בַּיּוֹם הַהוּא
the splendor	הַהוֹד
that	הַהִיא
those	הָהֵם
the mountains	הֶהָרִים
he, it	הוּא
that	הַהוּא
on that day	בַּיּוֹם הַהוּא
when he, when it	כְּשֶׁהוּא
that he, that it	שֶׁהוּא
thanks	הוֹדָאוֹת
Give thanks! Praise!	הוֹדוּ
thanking, praising	הוֹדוֹת, הֹדוֹת
he is (very rarely used)	הֹוֶה
Save us!	הוֹשִׁיעֵנוּ
Save!	הוֹשַׁע
this	הַזֹּאת
this	הַזֶּה
the one who remembers	הַזּוֹכֵר
the rememberance	הַזִּכָּרוֹן
the month	הַחֹדֶשׁ
life	הַחַיִּים
loving-kindness	הַחֶסֶד
the darkness	הַחֹשֶׁךְ
the good one, good	הַטּוֹב
the goodness, good	הַטּוֹבָה
the good ones, good	הַטּוֹבִים
she, it	הִיא
that	הַהִיא
that it	שֶׁהִיא
the hand	הַיָּד
(he) was, (it) was	הָיָה
may (it) be, (it) will be	וְהָיָה
as it was	כְּשֶׁהָיָה
who was, that was	שֶׁהָיָה
(they) were	הָיוּ
may (they) be, (they) will be	וְהָיוּ
that were	שֶׁהָיוּ

To find a word:

- Disregard וְ, וּ, וַ, וָ, וֶ or וִ, (meaning **and**) at the beginning of a word.
- Disregard the dot in the center of letters.
- Check "The Names of God" which are listed separately beginning on page 75.
- Insert **am, is, are** wherever needed to make sense of a sentence in English.

א ב ג ד ה ו ז ח ט י כ ל מ נ ס ע פ צ ק ר ש ת

הַיּוֹם	today, the day
הַיּוֹצֵר	the one who forms
הַיָּם	the sea
הַיָּמִים	the days
הַיְשׁוּעָה	the deliverance
הַכָּבוֹד	glory, the glory
הַכֹּל	all, everything
הַכַּלָּה	the bride
הַכָּתוּב	the writing
הַלֵּב	the heart
הַלֵּבָב	the heart
הַלַּיְלָה	the night, tonight
הַלֵּילוֹת	the nights, nights
הַלְלוּהוּ	praise him
הֵם	they
הָהֵם	those
הַמְבָרֵךְ	the one who blesses
הַמְבֹרָךְ	the blessed one
הַמָּגֵן	the shield
הֲמוֹנָם	their multitudes
הַמּוֹצִיא	the one who brings forth
הַמּוֹשִׁיעַ	the one who saves
הַמְיַחֲדִים	the ones who proclaim the unity of
הַמַּיִם	the water
הִמְלִיכוּ	(they) caused (someone) to be king
הַמֶּלֶךְ	the king
הַמַּלְכוּת	the kingdom
הַמְּלָכִים	the kings
מֶלֶךְ מַלְכֵי הַמְּלָכִים	the king of the kings of the kings *(Idiom)*
הַמַּמְלָכָה	the kingdom
הַמְּנוּחָה	the rest, the tranquility
הַמַּעֲשֶׂה	the deed, creation
הַמַּצְמִיחַ	the one who causes to spring forth
הַמַּקְדִּישִׁים	the ones who make holy
הַמָּקוֹם	the place
הַמְקַיֵּם	the one who keeps

To find a word:

- Disregard וְ, וּ, וַ, וָ, וֶ or וִ, (meaning **and**) at the beginning of a word.
- Disregard the dot in the center of letters.
- Check "The Names of God" which are listed separately beginning on page 75.
- Insert **am, is, are** wherever needed to make sense of a sentence in English.

א ב ג ד ה ו ז ח ט י כ ל מ נ ס ע פ צ ק ר ש ת

הַמְרַחֵם	the compassionate one
הַמִּשְׁפָּט	the judgement
הַמִּשְׂרָה	the rule
הַמֵּתִים	the dead
הַמַּתִּיר	the one who sets free
הַמִּתְנַשֵּׂא	the exaltedness
הַנֶּאֱמָן	faithful, the faithful
הִנֵּא	Behold! See!
הַנּוֹפְלִים	the fallen
הַנּוֹרָא	the awesome one
הַנּוֹתֵן	the one who gives
הִנְחִילָנוּ	(he) gave us as an inheritance
הִנְחַלְתָּנוּ	you have given us as an inheritance
הַנֵּצַח	the victory
הַסּוֹמֵךְ	the one who supports
הָעוֹלָם	eternity, the universe
הָעוֹלָמִים	eternity, the universe
הָעוֹשֵׂה	the one who does, the one who makes
הָעֹז	the strength
הָעֶלְיוֹן	the highest
הָעָם	the people
הָעַמִּים	the peoples
הָעֹמֶר	the Omer, an ancient grain measure, or the days counted between Passover and Shavuot
הֶעָפָר	the dust
הָעֹשֶׂה	the one who does, the one who makes
הַצַּדִּיק	the righteous one, righteous
הַצַּדִּיקִים	the righteous, the righteous ones
הַצֶּדֶק	the righteousness, righteousness
הַצְּדָקָה	the righteousness
הַצּוּר	the rock
הַצָּרָה	the trouble, the distress
הַקָּדוֹשׁ	the holy one
הַקְּדוֹשִׁים	the holy ones
הַקֹּדֶשׁ	holiness, the holy place

To find a word:

- Disregard וְ, וּ, וַ, וָ, וֶ or וִ, (meaning **and**) at the beginning of a word.
- Disregard the dot in the center of letters.
- Check "The Names of God" which are listed separately beginning on page 75.
- Insert **am, is, are** wherever needed to make sense of a sentence in English.

ה־ו

א ב ג ד ה ו ז ח ט י כ ל מ נ ס ע פ צ ק ר ש ת

mountain, the mountain of	הַר
on the mountain of	בְּהַר
as the mountain of	כְּהַר
toward the mountain of	לְהַר
from the mountain of	מֵהַר
numerous	הָרָב
the many, many	הָרַבִּים
the spirit, the breath	הָרוּחַ
the one who cures	הָרוֹפֵא
the compassion	הָרַחֲמִים
the compassionate one	הָרַחֲמָן
mountains	הָרִים
in the mountains	בֶּהָרִים
the mountains	הֶהָרִים
raise	הָרֵם
the evil, evil	הָרָע
the evil, evil	הָרָעָה
the wicked ones	הָרְשָׁעִים
the seventh	הַשְּׁבִיעִי
the Sabbath	הַשַּׁבָּת
you reflected	הֲשֵׁבֹתָ
and may you reflect, and you shall reflect	וַהֲשֵׁבֹתָ
the one who keeps, the one who guards	הַשּׁוֹמֵר
cause us to return	הֲשִׁיבֵנוּ
the song	הַשִּׁיר
the peace, peace	הַשָּׁלוֹם
the name, a way of referring to God	הַשֵּׁם
the heavens	הַשָּׁמַיִם
the year	הַשָּׁנָה
the sixth	הַשִּׁשִּׁי
the Torah	הַתּוֹרָה
the glory	הַתִּפְאֶרֶת

ו

and (always attached to the beginning of a word)	וְ, וּ, וָ, וַ, וֶ, וֵ
and may you love, and you shall love	וְאָהַבְתָּ
and may you speak, and you shall speak	וְדִבַּרְתָּ

To find a word:

- Disregard וָ, וּ, וַ, וָ, וֶ or וֵ, (meaning **and**) at the beginning of a word.
- Disregard the dot in the center of letters.
- Check "The Names of God" which are listed separately beginning on page 75.
- Insert **am, is, are** wherever needed to make sense of a sentence in English.

and may (it) be, and (it) shall be . . . . וְהָיָה

and may (they) be, and (they) shall be . . וְהָיוּ

and may you reflect, and you shall reflect . . . . וַהֲשֵׁבֹתָ

and (he) blessed . . . . וַיְבָרֶךְ

and you will know . . . . וְיָדַעְתָּ

and there was . . . . וַיְהִי

and (they) were . . . . וַיִּהְיוּ

and (he) finished . . . . וַיְכַל

and (they) were finished . . . . וַיְכֻלּוּ

and (he) ruled . . . . וַיִּמְלֹךְ

and (he) rested . . . . וַיִּנָּפַשׁ

and (he) made holy . . . . וַיְקַדֵּשׁ

and (he) ceased work, and (he) rested . וַיִּשְׁבֹּת

and may you write them, and you shall write them . . . . . וּכְתַבְתָּם

and ever . . . . וָעֶד

  forever and ever *(Idiom)* . . לְעוֹלָם וָעֶד

and (he) commanded us . . . . וְצִוָּנוּ

and may you bind them, and you shall bind them . . . . . . וּקְשַׁרְתָּם

and may (they) keep, and (they) shall keep . . . . וְשָׁמְרוּ

and may you teach them, and you shall teach them . . . . . . וְשִׁנַּנְתָּם

ז

this . . . . זֹאת

  with this . . . . בְּזֹאת

  this . . . . הַזֹּאת

this . . . . זֶה

  with this . . . . בָּזֶה

  this . . . . הַזֶּה

  from this . . . . מִזֶּה

one to another *(Idiom)* . . . . זֶה אֶל זֶה

one to another *(Idiom)* . . . . זֶה לָזֶה

remember, (one) who remembers . . . זוֹכֵר

  the one who remembers . . . . . הַזּוֹכֵר

other than him . . . . זוּלָתוֹ

a memory, the memory of . . . . זֵכֶר

  to the memory of . . . . לְזֵכֶר

remembrance . . . . זִכָּרוֹן, זִכְרוֹן

  the remembrance . . . . הַזִּכָּרוֹן

  for a remembrance, in memory of לְזִכָּרוֹן

To find a word:

- Disregard וְ, וּ, וַ, וָ, וֶ or וֵ, (meaning **and**) at the beginning of a word.
- Disregard the dot in the center of letters.
- Check "The Names of God" which are listed separately beginning on page 75.
- Insert **am, is, are** wherever needed to make sense of a sentence in English.

אבגדהוזחטיכלמנסעפצקרשת

sin . . . חֵטְא
- for the sin *(Idiom)* . . . עַל חֵטְא

we have sinned . . . חָטָאנוּ
- that we have sinned . . . שֶׁחָטָאנוּ

living, living thing . . . חַי

the life of . . . חַיֵּי
- in the lives of . . . *(Aramaic)* בְּחַיֵּי

eternal life *(Idiom)* . . . חַיֵּי עוֹלָם

life . . . חַיִּים
- life, in life . . . בַּחַיִּים
- life . . . הַחַיִּים
- to life . . . לְחַיִּים
- a tree of life *(Idiom)* . . . עֵץ חַיִּים

our lives . . . חַיֵּינוּ

challah, Sabbath or holiday bread . . . חַלָּה

our share, our portion . . . חֶלְקֵנוּ

Have compassion! . . . חֲמוֹל

chometz, bread, not kosher for Passover . . . חָמֵץ

grace, favor . . . חֵן
- with grace, with favor . . . בְּחֵן

gracious, kind . . . חַנּוּן

remember us . . . זָכְרֵנוּ

time, season . . . זְמַן
- in the season . . . בַּזְּמַן
- in a time . . . בִּזְמַן
- at this season *(Idiom)* . . . בַּזְּמַן הַזֶּה
- to this season *(Idiom)* . . . לַזְּמַן הַזֶּה

my pain . . . חֶבְלִי

holiday, the holiday of . . . חַג, חָג
- on the holiday of . . . בְּחַג

Make new! . . . חַדֵּשׁ

month . . . חֹדֶשׁ
- in the month . . . בַּחֹדֶשׁ
- in the month of . . . בְּחֹדֶשׁ
- the month . . . הַחֹדֶשׁ
- of the month . . . לַחֹדֶשׁ

new . . . חֲדָשָׁה

the sick . . . חוֹלִים

cantor . . . חַזָּן

strong . . . חָזָק

To find a word:
- Disregard וְ, וּ, וַ, וָ, וֶ or וִ, (meaning **and**) at the beginning of a word.
- Disregard the dot in the center of letters.
- Check "The Names of God" which are listed separately beginning on page 75.
- Insert **am, is, are** wherever needed to make sense of a sentence in English.

א ב ג ד ה ו ז ח ט י כ ל מ נ ס ע פ צ ק ר ש ת

Chanukah, festival of lights . . . . חֲנֻכָּה

Chanukah menorah . . . . חֲנֻכִּיָּה

favor us . . . . חָנֵּנוּ

loving-kindness, loving-kindness of . . . חֶסֶד

with loving-kindness . . . . בְּחֶסֶד

loving-kindness . . . . הַחֶסֶד

his loving-kindness . . . . חַסְדּוֹ

because his loving-kindness is forever *(Idiom)* . . כִּי לְעוֹלָם חַסְדּוֹ

the kindnesses of . . . . חַסְדֵי

loving-kindness, the kind ones . . . . חֲסָדִים

your loving-kindness . . . . . חַסְדְּךָ, חַסְדֵּךְ

in your loving-kindness, with your loving-kindness בְּחַסְדְּךָ, בְּחַסְדֵּךְ

according to your loving-kindness . . . כְּחַסְדְּךָ, כְּחַסְדֵּךְ

sword . . . . חֶרֶב

becomes angry, will become angry *(Idiom)* . . . . חָרָה אַף

darkness . . . . חֹשֶׁךְ

in the darkness . . . . בַּחֹשֶׁךְ

the darkness . . . . הַחֹשֶׁךְ

darkness, to darkness . . . . לְחֹשֶׁךְ

from darkness . . . . מֵחֹשֶׁךְ

ט

Tu B'shevat, festival celebrating the planting of trees . . . . . . ט״ו בִּשְׁבָט

good, it is good . . . . טוֹב

in goodness . . . . בַּטּוֹב

the good one, good . . . . הַטּוֹב

for the good, good . . . . לַטּוֹב

for good, good . . . . לְטוֹב

goodness, good . . . . טוֹבָה, טֹבָה

the goodness, good . . . . הַטּוֹבָה

for goodness . . . . לְטוֹבָה

good . . . . טוֹבִים

the good ones, good . . . . . . הַטּוֹבִים

for the good ones . . . . לַטּוֹבִים

your goodness . . . . טוּבְךָ, טוּבֵךְ

in your goodness . . . בְּטוּבְךָ, בְּטוּבֵךְ

from your goodness . . מִטּוּבְךָ, מִטּוּבֵךְ

tallit, tallis, prayer shawl . . . . טַלִּית

our children, our little ones . . . . טַפֵּנוּ

To find a word:

- Disregard וְ, וּ, וַ, וָ, וֶ or וֵ, (meaning **and**) at the beginning of a word.
- Disregard the dot in the center of letters.
- Check "The Names of God" which are listed separately beginning on page 75.
- Insert **am, is, are** wherever needed to make sense of a sentence in English.

א ב ג ד ה ו ז ח ט י כ ל מ נ ס ע פ צ ק ר ש ת

י

יֹאמְרוּ (they) will say

יָבוֹא, יָבֹא (he) will come
- שֶׁיָּבֹא that will come

יְבָרֵךְ, יְבָרֶךְ (he) will bless
- וַיְבָרֶךְ and (he) blessed

יַגִּיד (he) will tell

יָד hand, pointer for Torah
- בְּיָד with a hand
- הַיָּד the hand
- מִיָּד from a hand

יַד the hand of
- בְּיַד through the hand of
- לְיַד near, at hand
- מִיַּד from the hand of

יְדֵי the hands of
- בִּידֵי in the hands of

יָדְךָ, יָדֶךָ your hand
- בְּיָדְךָ, בְּיָדֶךָ in your hand, in your hands

יֵדְעוּ (they) will know

יָדַעְתָּ you knew
- וְיָדַעְתָּ and you will know

יְהֵא *(Aramaic)* let it be

יְהוּדָה Judah
- לִיהוּדָה to Judah, for Judah

יְהִי it will be, let it be
- וַיְהִי and there was

יִהְיֶה (he) will be, (it) will be

יִהְיוּ (they) will be
- וַיִּהְיוּ and (they) were
- כְּשֶׁיִּהְיוּ when (they) will be
- שֶׁיִּהְיוּ that (they) will be

יְהַלְלוּךָ (they) will praise you

יוֹדוּךָ, יוֹדֶךָ (they) will thank you

יוֹם day, the day of
- בַּיּוֹם on the day
- בְּיוֹם on the day of
- הַיּוֹם today, the day
- כַּיּוֹם as the day
- כְּיוֹם as a day, on the day of
- לַיּוֹם for the day
- לְיוֹם for the day of
- מִיּוֹם from the day, from the day of

To find a word:
- Disregard וְ, וּ, וַ, וָ, וֶ or וִ, (meaning **and**) at the beginning of a word.
- Disregard the dot in the center of letters.
- Check "The Names of God" which are listed separately beginning on page 75.
- Insert **am, is, are** wherever needed to make sense of a sentence in English.

א ב ג ד ה ו ז ח ט י כ ל מ נ ס ע פ צ ק ר ש ת

- **יוֹם כִּפּוּר** — Yom Kippur, the day of atonement
- **יוֹסֵד** — founds, (one) who founds
- **יוֹצֵר** — forms, (one) who forms
  - הַיּוֹצֵר — the one who forms
  - לְיוֹצֵר — to the one who forms
- **יוֹשְׁבֵי, יֹשְׁבֵי** — those who live
- **יוֹשְׁבִין** — sitting
- **יַחַד** — together
- **יָחֹן** — may (he) favor
- **יַכִּירוּ** — (they) will recognize
- **יְכַל** — (he) will finish
  - וַיְכַל — and (he) finished
- **יְכֻלּוּ** — (they) will be finished
  - וַיְכֻלּוּ — and (they) were finished
- **יִכְרְעוּ** — (they) will bend (the knee)
- **יָם** — sea, the sea of
  - בַּיָּם — in the sea
  - הַיָּם — the sea
  - כַּיָּם — as the sea
- **יָמוּשׁ** — (he) will depart, (it) will depart

- **יְמֵי** — the days of
  - בִּימֵי — in the days of
  - כִּימֵי — as the days of
  - מִימֵי — from the days of
- **יָמִים** — days
  - בַּיָּמִים — in the days
  - בַּיָּמִים הָהֵם — in those days *(Idiom)*
  - הַיָּמִים — the days
  - מִיָּמִים — after awhile
- **יָמֵינוּ** — our days
  - בְּיָמֵינוּ — in our days
- **יְמִינְךָ, יְמִינֶךָ** — your right hand
  - בִּימִינְךָ, בִּימִינֶךָ — with your right hand
  - מִימִינְךָ, מִימִינֶךָ — as your right hand
- **יִמְלוֹךְ, יִמְלֹךְ** — (he) will rule, may (he) rule
  - וַיִּמְלֹךְ — and (he) ruled
- **יַמְלִיךְ** *(Aramaic)* — (he) will rule
- **יִנָּפֵשׁ** — (he) will rest
  - וַיִּנָּפַשׁ — and (he) rested
- **יַעֲמֹד** — (he) will stand
- **יַעֲקֹב, יַעֲקוֹב** — Jacob
  - בְּיַעֲקֹב — with Jacob
  - לְיַעֲקֹב — to Jacob
  - מִיַּעֲקֹב — from Jacob

To find a word:

- Disregard וְ, וּ, וַ, וָ, וֶ or וִ, (meaning **and**) at the beginning of a word.
- Disregard the dot in the center of letters.
- Check "The Names of God" which are listed separately beginning on page 75.
- Insert **am, is, are** wherever needed to make sense of a sentence in English.

י

יַעֲשֶׂה . . . . may (he) make, (he) will make, (he) will do

- שֶׁיַּעֲשֶׂה . . . . that (he) will make, that (he) will do

יִפְּלוּ . . . . (they) will fall

יִפֶן . . . . may (he) turn, (he) will turn

יִצְחָק . . . . Isaac

- לְיִצְחָק . . . . to Isaac

יְצִיר . . . . creature

יְקַבְּלוּ may (they) receive, (they) shall receive

יְקַדֵּשׁ . . . . (he) will make holy

- וַיְקַדֵּשׁ . . . . and (he) made holy

יְקָר . . . . splendor

יִקְרְאוּ . . . . (they) will call, may (they) call

יְקָרוֹ . . . . his splendor

יִרְאָה . . . . awe

- בְּיִרְאָה . . . . with awe
- לְיִרְאָה . . . . to be in awe of

יְרוּשָׁלַיִם, יְרוּשָׁלָיִם, יְרוּשָׁלֶם Jerusalem

- בִּירוּשָׁלַיִם . . . . in Jerusalem
- כִּירוּשָׁלַיִם . . . . as Jerusalem
- לִירוּשָׁלַיִם . . . . to Jerusalem
- מִירוּשָׁלַיִם . . . . from Jerusalem

יְרָקוֹת . . . . greens, vegetables

יֹשְׁבֵי, יוֹשְׁבֵי . . . . those who live

יִשְׁבֹּת . . (he) will cease work, (he) will rest

- וַיִּשְׁבֹּת . . . . . . and (he) ceased work, and (he) rested

יְשׁוּעָה . . . . deliverance

- בִּישׁוּעָה . . . . with deliverance
- הַיְשׁוּעָה . . . . the deliverance
- לִישׁוּעָה . . . . for deliverance

יְשׁוּעָתְךָ, יְשׁוּעָתֶךָ . . . your deliverance

- בִּישׁוּעָתְךָ, בִּישׁוּעָתֶךָ . . . . in your deliverance
- לִישׁוּעָתְךָ, לִישׁוּעָתֶךָ . . . . for your deliverance

יַשְׁמִיעֵנוּ . . . . (he) will make us hear

יִשְׁעֵנוּ . . . . our deliverer, our keeper

יִשְׁתַּבַּח *(Aramaic)* . . . . praised

יִשְׂרָאֵל . . . . Israel

- בְּיִשְׂרָאֵל . . . . in Israel
- לְיִשְׂרָאֵל . . . . . to Israel, for Israel

יִתְבָּרַךְ *(Aramaic)* . . . . blessed

יִתְגַּדַּל *(Aramaic)* . . . . great

יִתְהַדָּר *(Aramaic)* . . . . . . grand, splendid

To find a word:

- Disregard וְ, וּ, וַ, וָ, וֶ or וִ, (meaning **and**) at the beginning of a word.
- Disregard the dot in the center of letters.
- Check "The Names of God" which are listed separately beginning on page 75.
- Insert **am, is, are** wherever needed to make sense of a sentence in English.

praised . . . . *(Aramaic)* יִתְהַלַּל

(he) will give, may (he) give . . . . יִתֵּן

let them give . . . . יִתְּנוּ

elevated . . . . *(Aramaic)* יִתְנַשֵּׂא

high . . . . *(Aramaic)* יִתְעַלֶּה

glorious . . . . *(Aramaic)* יִתְפָּאַר

holy . . . . *(Aramaic)* יִתְקַדַּשׁ

exalted . . . . *(Aramaic)* יִתְרוֹמַם

כ

as, like . . . . כְּ, כַּ, כָּ, כֶּ, כִּ, כֵּ
(always attached to the beginning of a word)

as a father . . . . כְּאָב

as man . . . . כְּאָדָם

as the light of . . . . כְּאוֹר

as one of, as one . . . . כְּאֶחָד

as a man, like a man, as a man of . . . כְּאִישׁ

like these . . . . כָּאֵלֶּה

like a fire . . . . כְּאֵשׁ

glory, honor . . . . כָּבוֹד

- in glory, in honor . . . . בְּכָבוֹד
- glory, the glory . . . . הַכָּבוֹד
- for glory, for honor . . . . לְכָבוֹד

the honor of, the glory of . . . . כְּבוֹד

- in honor of . . . . לִכְבוֹד

his glory, his honor . . . . כְּבוֹדוֹ

- in his glory . . . . בִּכְבוֹדוֹ

your glory . . . . כְּבוֹדֶךָ

- in your glory . . . . בִּכְבוֹדֶךָ

as the children of . . . . כִּבְנֵי

as strong, as a mighty one . . . . . . כְּגִבּוֹר

as the nations of . . . . כְּגוֹיֵי

according to the word . . . . כַּדָּבָר

according to the word of . . . . כִּדְבַר

as theirs . . . . כָּהֶם

Cohen, priest . . . . כֹּהֵן

as the mountain of . . . . כְּהַר

To find a word:

- Disregard וְ, וּ, וַ, וָ, וֶ or וִ, (meaning **and**) at the beginning of a word.
- Disregard the dot in the center of letters.
- Check "The Names of God" which are listed separately beginning on page 75.
- Insert **am, is, are** wherever needed to make sense of a sentence in English.

א ב ג ד ה ו ז ח ט י כ ל מ נ ס ע פ צ ק ר ש ת

- all of, any . . . כָּל
  - in all of, with all of, in every . . . בְּכָל
  - according to all of . . . כְּכָל
  - to all of . . . לְכָל
  - from all of . . . מִכָּל
  - that on all of, that on every . . . שֶׁבְּכָל
- all, everything . . . כֹּל
  - with all, over all . . . בַּכֹּל
  - all, everything . . . הַכֹּל
  - according to all of . . . כְּכֹל
  - to all . . . לַכֹּל
  - to all . . . לְכֹל
  - from all . . . מִכֹּל
  - that all . . . שֶׁהַכֹּל
- bride . . . כַּלָּה
  - the bride . . . הַכַּלָּה
  - as a bride . . . כַּכַּלָּה
- make an end to . . . כַּלֵּה
- all of it, all . . . כֻּלּוֹ
- all of them . . . כֻּלָּם, כּוּלָּם
  - to all of them . . . לְכֻלָּם
  - from all of them . . . מִכֻּלָּם
  - that all of them . . . שֶׁכֻּלָּם
- all of us . . . כֻּלָּנוּ

- all of them . . . כּוּלָּם, כֻּלָּם
- my cup . . . כּוֹסִי
- bend the knees . . . כּוֹרְעִים
- according to your loving-kindness . . . כְּחַסְדְּךָ, כְּחַסְדֶּךָ
- that, because, when, but, as . . . כִּי
- because his loving-kindness is forever *(Idiom)* . . . כִּי לְעוֹלָם חַסְדּוֹ
- as the day . . . כַּיּוֹם
- as a day, on the day of . . . כְּיוֹם
- as the sea . . . כַּיָּם
- as the days of . . . כִּימֵי
- as Jerusalem . . . כִּירוּשָׁלַיִם
- according to all of . . . כְּכָל
- according to all of . . . כְּכֹל
- as a bride . . . כַּכַּלָּה
- the finishing of . . . כִּכְלוֹת
- as it is written . . . כַּכָּתוּב

To find a word:

- Disregard וְ, וּ, וַ, וָ, וֶ or וֵ, (meaning **and**) at the beginning of a word.
- Disregard the dot in the center of letters.
- Check "The Names of God" which are listed separately beginning on page 75.
- Insert **am, is, are** wherever needed to make sense of a sentence in English.

א ב ג ד ה ו ז ח ט י כ ל מ נ ס ע פ צ ק ר ש ת

like, as	כְּמוֹ
like you	כָּמוֹךָ, כָּמוֹכָה
like our saviour	כְּמוֹשִׁיעֵנוּ
as our king, like our king	כְּמַלְכֵּנוּ
as your works	כְּמַעֲשֶׂיךָ
as Moses	כְּמשֶׁה
as the families of	כְּמִשְׁפְּחוֹת
thus, indeed	כֵּן
thus	בְּכֵן
therefore *(Idiom)*	עַל כֵּן
as you promised	כִּנְאֻמֶךָ
according to the mystic saying of *(Idiom)*	כְּסוֹד שִׂיחַ
like your people	כְּעַמְּךָ, כְּעַמֶּךָ
as dust	כֶּעָפָר
kipa, skullcap, yarmulke	כִּפָּה
as my mouth, as the mouth of, according to	כְּפִי
Atone!	כַּפֵּר
as of old	כְּקֶדֶם
(will be) utterly destroyed *(Idiom)*	כָּרוֹת יִכָּרֵתוּן
as (one) has compassion	כְּרַחֵם
according to his will *(Aramaic)*	כִּרְעוּתֵהּ
when man	כְּשֶׁאָדָם
when I	כְּשֶׁאֲנִי
when you	כְּשֶׁאַתָּה
when he, when it	כְּשֶׁהוּא
when it was	כְּשֶׁהָיָה
when (they) will be	כְּשֶׁיִּהְיוּ
when to you, as yours, when you	כְּשֶׁלָּךְ
as the name of, just as the name	כְּשֵׁם
as his name	כִּשְׁמוֹ
as your name	כְּשִׁמְךָ, כְּשִׁמֶךָ
Kosher, ritually proper	כָּשֵׁר
write us down	כָּתְבֵנוּ
you wrote them	כְּתַבְתָּם
may you write them, you shall write them	וּכְתַבְתָּם

To find a word:
- Disregard וְ, וּ, וַ, וָ, וֶ or וִ, (meaning **and**) at the beginning of a word.
- Disregard the dot in the center of letters.
- Check "The Names of God" which are listed separately beginning on page 75.
- Insert **am, is, are** wherever needed to make sense of a sentence in English.

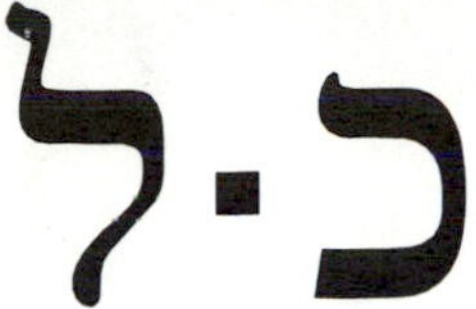

א ב ג ד ה ו ז ח ט י כ ל מ נ ס ע פ צ ק ר ש ת

כָּתוּב	written
הַכָּתוּב	the writing
כַּכָּתוּב	as it is written
כְּתוּבָּה	Ketuba, marriage contract
כַּתּוֹרָה	according to the law, according to the Torah

לְ, לַ, לָ, לֶ, לִ, לֹ	to, for, toward (always attached to the beginning of a word)
לֹא	not, do not
בְּלֹא	without
שֶׁלֹּא	that not, who not
לַאֲבוֹתֵינוּ	to our fathers, ancestors, for our fathers, ancestors
לְאַבְרָהָם	to Abraham
לַאֲדוֹן	to the master of
לְאָדָם	to man
לֵאָה	Leah
לְאוֹת	as a sign, as the sign of
לְאֵין	without
לְאִישׁ	as a man, to a man, for a man of
לָאֵלֶּה	to these
לֵאמֹר	saying
לָאָרֶץ	to the land, for the land
לַאֲשֶׁר	to that which, to wherever
לֵב	heart, the heart of
בְּלֵב	in the heart of
הַלֵּב	the heart
לֵבָב	heart
בְּלֵבָב	with a heart
הַלֵּבָב	the heart
לְבַב	the heart of
לְבָבְךָ, לְבָבֵךְ	your heart
לְבַדּוֹ	alone
לִבִּי	my heart
בְּלִבִּי	in my heart
לְבֵית	to the house of
לְבֵיתְךָ, לְבֵיתֵךְ	to your house, for your house, for your household

To find a word:

- Disregard וְ, וּ, וַ, וָ, וֶ or וִ, (meaning **and**) at the beginning of a word.
- Disregard the dot in the center of letters.
- Check "The Names of God" which are listed separately beginning on page 75.
- Insert **am, is, are** wherever needed to make sense of a sentence in English.

ל

א ב ג ד ה ו ז ח ט י כ ל מ נ ס ע פ צ ק ר ש ת

their hearts	לִבָּם
to the son, to the son of	לְבֶן
our hearts	לִבֵּנוּ
in our hearts	בְּלִבֵּנוּ
to the children of	לִבְנֵי
to their children, for their children	לִבְנֵיהֶם
to your children	לְבָנֶיךָ
in the morning	לַבֹּקֶר
for the covenant, for the pledge	לַבְּרִית
for the covenant of, for the pledge of	לִבְרִית
to bless, to praise	לְבָרֵךְ
for a blessing	לִבְרָכָה
as flesh	לְבָשָׂר
to the nations	לַגּוֹיִם
of David, to David	לְדָוִד
to my beloved, for my beloved	לְדוֹדִי
from generation to generation, for all generations *(Idiom)*	לְדוֹר וָדוֹר
to know	לָדַעַת
for their generations	לְדֹרֹתָם
to light	לְהַדְלִיק
to give thanks	לְהוֹדוֹת
to save	לְהוֹשִׁיעַ
to join to	לְהַחְבִּירָה
to revive	לְהַחֲיוֹת
to be	לִהְיוֹת
to them, for them, them	לָהֶם
to compare	לְהַמְשִׁיל
to remove	לְהַעֲבִיר
to turn	לְהַפְנוֹת
toward the mountain of	לְהַר
to him, for him, him	לוֹ
Levi, Levite	לֵוִי
Lulav, palm branch used in celebration of Succot (סֻכּוֹת)	לוּלָב
to the memory of	לְזֵכֶר
for a remembrance, in memory of	לְזִכָּרוֹן

To find a word:

- Disregard וְ, וּ, וַ, וָ, וֶ or וֵ, (meaning **and**) at the beginning of a word.
- Disregard the dot in the center of letters.
- Check "The Names of God" which are listed separately beginning on page 75.
- Insert **am, is, are** wherever needed to make sense of a sentence in English.

א ב ג ד ה ו ז ח ט י כ ל מ נ ס ע פ צ ק ר ש ת

to this season (*Idiom*)	לַזְּמַן הַזֶּה
of the month	לַחֹדֶשׁ
to life	לַחַיִּים
bread	לֶחֶם
darkness, to darkness	לְחֹשֶׁךְ
for the good, good	לַטּוֹב
for good, good	לְטוֹב
for goodness	לְטוֹבָה
for the good ones	לַטּוֹבִים
as a reminder, as a symbol	לְטֹטָפֹת
to me, for me, me	לִי
near, at hand	לְיַד
to Judah, for Judah	לִיהוּדָה
for the day	לַיּוֹם
for the day of	לְיוֹם
to the one who forms	לְיוֹצֵר
night	לַיְלָה, לָיְלָה
at night	בַּלַּיְלָה
the night, tonight	הַלַּיְלָה
to Jacob	לְיַעֲקֹב
to Isaac	לְיִצְחָק
of the Exodus from	לִיצִיאַת
to be in awe of	לְיִרְאָה
to Jerusalem	לִירוּשָׁלַיִם
for deliverance	לִישׁוּעָה
for your deliverance	לִישׁוּעָתְךָ, לִישׁוּעָתֵךְ
to those who sleep in	לִישֵׁנֵי
to Israel, for Israel	לְיִשְׂרָאֵל
to you, for you, you, yours	לְךָ
as yours, when you	כְּשֶׁלְּךָ
yours	שֶׁלְּךָ
to you, for you, you, yours	לָךְ
yours	שֶׁלָּךְ
in honor of	לִכְבוֹד
for glory, for honor	לְכָבוֹד
come, to you, yours	לְכָה
come my beloved (*Idiom*)	לְכָה דוֹדִי
to all	לַכֹּל

To find a word:

- Disregard וְ, וּ, וַ, וָ, וֶ or וֵ, (meaning **and**) at the beginning of a word.
- Disregard the dot in the center of letters.
- Check "The Names of God" which are listed separately beginning on page 75.
- Insert **am, is, are** wherever needed to make sense of a sentence in English.

ל

א ב ג ד ה ו ז ח ט י כ ל מ נ ס ע פ צ ק ר ש ת

לְכָל	to all of
לְכֹל	to all
לְכֻלָּם	to all of them
לָכֶם	to you, for you, you
לְמוֹשִׁיעֵנוּ	to our saviour
לַמַּחֲזִיקִים	for those who grasp
לַמֶּלֶךְ	to the king
לְמֶלֶךְ	as king, to the king of
לְמַלְכוּתְךָ, לְמַלְכוּתֶךָ	to your kingdom
לַמְּלָכִים	to kings
לְמַלְכֵּנוּ	to our king
לִמְנוּחָה	for rest
לְמַעַן	in order to, for the sake of
לְמַעֲשֵׂה	to the doing of, to the work of, for the doing of, for the work of
לְמִצְוֹתָיו	to his commandments
לְמִצְוֹתֶיךָ	to your commandments, for your commandments
לַמָּקוֹם	the place, to the place
לְמִקְרָאֵי קֹדֶשׁ	for the holy festivals *(Idiom)*
לַמָּרוֹם	on high
לְמֹשֶׁה	to Moses, for Moses
לְמִשְׁפָּט	for justice, with justice
לָנוּ	to us, for us, us
לְנַפְשִׁי	to my soul, for my soul
לְנֵצַח נְצָחִים	forever and ever *(Idiom)*
לְעַבְדְּךָ, לְעַבְדֶּךָ	to your servant, for your servant
לָעַד	forever
לְעוֹלָם, לְעֹלָם, לָעוֹלָם	forever
לְעוֹלָם וָעֶד	forever and ever *(Idiom)*
לְעוֹלְמֵי עַד	forever and ever *(Idiom)*
לְעוֹלָמִים	forever
לְעוֹשֵׂה	to the doer of, to the maker of
לְעֵינֵי	before the eyes of
לְעֵינֵינוּ	before our eyes
לְעֵלָּא	above *(Aramaic)*

To find a word:

- Disregard וְ, וּ, וַ, וָ, וֶ or וִ, (meaning **and**) at the beginning of a word.
- Disregard the dot in the center of letters.
- Check "The Names of God" which are listed separately beginning on page 75.
- Insert **am, is, are** wherever needed to make sense of a sentence in English.

א ב ג ד ה ו ז ח ט י כ ל מ נ ס ע פ צ ק ר ש ת

before, in front of	לִפְנֵי
from before	מִלִּפְנֵי
before him	לְפָנָיו
before you, in front of you	לְפָנֶיךָ
from before you	מִלְּפָנֶיךָ
for the righteous one, to the righteous	לַצַּדִּיק
for the righteous, to the righteous	לַצַּדִּיקִים
for righteousness	לִצְדָקָה
to the rock of	לְצוּר
to Zion	לְצִיּוֹן
for the holy place	לַקֹּדֶשׁ
his holy place, to his holy place	לְקָדְשׁוֹ
to the voice of	לְקוֹל
to meet, towards	לִקְרַאת
to the near one, to the near	לַקָּרוֹב
to see	לִרְאוֹת
as a head, as the head of	לְרֹאשׁ
to have compassion	לְרַחֵם

forever *(Aramaic)*	לְעָלַם
forever and ever *(Aramaic Idiom)*	לְעָלַם וּלְעָלְמֵי עָלְמַיָּא
forever *(Aramaic)*	לְעָלְמֵי
to the people	לָעָם
as a people, to a people, as the people of, to the people of	לְעָם, לְעַם
to his people	לְעַמּוֹ
to your people, your people	לְעַמְּךָ, לְעַמֶּךָ
of the Omer, an ancient grain measure, the days counted between Passover and Shavuot	לָעֹמֶר
toward	לְעֻמַּת
toward them	לְעֻמָּתָם
to the dust	לֶעָפָר
as dust	לְעָפָר
to the doer of, to the maker of	לְעֹשֵׂה
to make, to do	לַעֲשׂוֹת
at the time of	לְעֵת
at my mouth, at the mouth of, according to	לְפִי

To find a word:

- Disregard וְ, וּ, וַ, וָ, וֶ or וֵ, (meaning **and**) at the beginning of a word.
- Disregard the dot in the center of letters.
- Check "The Names of God" which are listed separately beginning on page 75.
- Insert **am, is, are** wherever needed to make sense of a sentence in English.

א ב ג ד ה ו ז ח ט י כ ל מ נ ס ע פ צ ק ר ש ת

for a good year, Happy New Year *(Idiom)*	לְשָׁנָה טוֹבָה
next year in Jerusalem *(Idiom)*	לְשָׁנָה הַבָּאָה בִּירוּשָׁלָיִם
for joy, for delight	לְשִׂמְחָה
for joy, for delight	לְשָׂשׂוֹן
for praise	לִתְהִלָּה
to the Torah	לַתּוֹרָה
for your Torah	לְתוֹרָתְךָ, לְתוֹרָתֵךְ
continually	לְתָמִיד
for glory, for the glory of	לְתִפְאֶרֶת
to repair	לְתַקֵּן
to give	לָתֵת

מ

from (always attached to the beginning of a word)	מִ, מֵ
very much, very	מְאֹד
your strength	מְאֹדֶךָ

compassion, for compassion	לְרַחֲמִים
for evil, evil	לָרָע
for evil, evil	לְרָעָה
favorable	לְרָצוֹן
for the wicked ones	לָרְשָׁעִים
to praise	לְשַׁבֵּחַ
the Sabbath	לַשַּׁבָּת
tongue	לָשׁוֹן
for peace, in peace	לְשָׁלוֹם
to complete	לְשַׁלֵּם
in the name of, for renown	לְשֵׁם
for your holy name *(Idiom)*	לְשֵׁם קָדְשֶׁךָ
to his name	לִשְׁמוֹ
to the heavens	לַשָּׁמַיִם
to your name	לִשְׁמְךָ, לִשְׁמֵךְ
to guard, to keep	לִשְׁמֹר
to the year	לְשָׁנָה

To find a word:

- Disregard וְ, וּ, וַ, וָ, וֶ or וִ, (meaning **and**) at the beginning of a word.
- Disregard the dot in the center of letters.
- Check "The Names of God" which are listed separately beginning on page 75.
- Insert **am, is, are** wherever needed to make sense of a sentence in English.

א ב ג ד ה ו ז ח ט י כ ל מ נ ס ע פ צ ק ר ש ת

מֵאָדָם	from man
מֵאָז	from that time
מֵאֵין	for want of
מֵאִישׁ	from man, from men of
מֵאֶרֶץ	from the land of
מֵאֵשׁ	from fire, by fire
מֵאֲשֶׁר	from which, from where
מְאֻשָּׁר	happy
מֵבִיא	bring, brings
מִבֵּין	from between, from among
מִבֵּית	from the house of
מִבְּנֵי	from among the children of
מְבָרַךְ	blessed (*Aramaic*)
מְבֹרָךְ	blessed, praised
הַמְבֹרָךְ	the blessed one
מִגּוֹי	from a nation
מָגֵן	who shields, shield of
הַמָּגֵן	the shield
מִדִּבְרֵי	by the words of
מַה, מָה	What? How!
בַּמָּה	How?
מֵהַר	from the mountain of
מְהֵרָה	quickly
בִּמְהֵרָה	quickly
מוֹדֶה	thank
מוֹדִים	thank
מוֹשַׁב	the seat of
מוֹשִׁיעַ	save, (one) who saves
הַמּוֹשִׁיעַ	the one who saves
מוֹשִׁיעֵנוּ	our saviour
כְּמוֹשִׁיעֵנוּ	like our saviour
לְמוֹשִׁיעֵנוּ	to our saviour
מִזֶּה	from this
מְזוּזָה	Mezuzah, encased scroll containing a section of Deuteronomy which is placed on doorposts
מְזֻזוֹת	doorposts, the doorposts of
מַזָּל טוֹב	mazel tov, good luck, congratulations (*Idiom*)

To find a word:

- Disregard וְ, וּ, וַ, וָ, וֶ or וִ, (meaning **and**) at the beginning of a word.
- Disregard the dot in the center of letters.
- Check "The Names of God" which are listed separately beginning on page 75.
- Insert **am, is, are** wherever needed to make sense of a sentence in English.

א	ב	ג	ד	ה	ו	ז	ח	ט	י	כ	ל	מ	נ	ס	ע	פ	צ	ק	ר	ש	ת

a psalm of David *(Idiom)*	מִזְמוֹר לְדָוִד
who gives life, who gives life to	מְחַיֵּה, מְחַיֶּה
Pardon!	מְחַל
from darkness	מֵחֹשֶׁךְ
dip	מַטְבִּילִין
from your goodness	מִטּוּבְךָ, מִטּוּבֶךָ
who	מִי
from a hand	מִיָּד
from the hand of	מִיַּד
from the day, from the day of	מִיּוֹם
water	מַיִם, מָיִם
in the water	בַּמַּיִם
in water	בְּמַיִם
the water	הַמַּיִם
from the days of	מִימֵי
after awhile, from the days	מִיָּמִים
as your right hand	מִימִינְךָ, מִימִינֶךָ
from Jacob	מִיַּעֲקֹב
from Jerusalem	מִירוּשָׁלַיִם
from all of	מִכָּל
from all	מִכֹּל
sustain, (one) who sustains	מְכַלְכֵּל
from all of them	מִכֻּלָּם
filled, was filled	מָלֵא
fills, full of	מְלֹא
the angels of	מַלְאֲכֵי
his work	מְלַאכְתּוֹ
(he) ruled	מָלַךְ
king, the king of	מֶלֶךְ
the king	הַמֶּלֶךְ
to the king	לַמֶּלֶךְ
as king, to the king of	לְמֶלֶךְ
from the king of	מִמֶּלֶךְ
that the king	שֶׁהַמֶּלֶךְ
the king of the kings of the kings *(Idiom)*	מֶלֶךְ מַלְכֵי הַמְּלָכִים
kingdom, the kingdom of	מַלְכוּת
in the kingdom of	בְּמַלְכוּת
the kingdom	הַמַּלְכוּת
his kingdom *(Aramaic)*	מַלְכוּתֵהּ
in his kingdom *(Aramaic)*	בְּמַלְכוּתֵהּ

To find a word:

- Disregard וְ, וּ, וַ, וָ, וֶ or וֵ, (meaning **and**) at the beginning of a word.
- Disregard the dot in the center of letters.
- Check "The Names of God" which are listed separately beginning on page 75.
- Insert **am, is, are** wherever needed to make sense of a sentence in English.

א ב ג ד ה ו ז ח ט י כ ל מ נ ס ע פ צ ק ר ש ת

his kingdom . . . . מַלְכוּתוֹ

your kingdom . . . . . מַלְכוּתְךָ, מַלְכוּתֶךָ
- in your kingdom . בְּמַלְכוּתְךָ, בְּמַלְכוּתֶךָ
- to your kingdom . לְמַלְכוּתְךָ, לְמַלְכוּתֶךָ

the kings of . . . . מַלְכֵי

kings . . . . מְלָכִים
- the kings . . . . הַמְּלָכִים
- to the kings . . . . לַמְּלָכִים

our king . . . . מַלְכֵּנוּ
- as our king, like our king . . . . כְּמַלְכֵּנוּ
- to our king . . . . לְמַלְכֵּנוּ

from before . . . . מִלְפְנֵי

from before you . . . . מִלְפָנֶיךָ

who brings death . . . . מֵמִית

from the king of . . . . מִמֶּלֶךְ

from him, from it, from us . . . . מִמֶּנּוּ
- that is from him, that is from it, that is from us . . . . שֶׁמִּמֶּנּוּ

above . . . . מִמַּעַל

from your commandments . . . . . מִמִּצְוֹתֶיךָ

from Egypt . . . . מִמִּצְרַיִם

from his place . . . . מִמְּקוֹמוֹ

from on high . . . . מִמָּרוֹם

your power . . . . מֶמְשַׁלְתְּךָ

from . . . . מִן

rest . . . . מְנוּחָה
- the rest . . . . הַמְּנוּחָה
- for rest . . . . לִמְנוּחָה

refuge . . . . מָנוֹס

Menorah, seven-branch candelabra . . מְנוֹרָה

Minyan, a quorum for public prayer, either ten men or ten people . . . מִנְיָן

my share of the cup *(Idiom)* . . . מְנָת כּוֹסִי

leaning, reclining . . . . מְסֵבִּין

from the earliest time . . . . מֵעוֹלָם

above . . . . מֵעַל

from me, against me . . . . מֵעָלַי

from upon us . . . . מֵעָלֵינוּ

from a people, from the people, from the people of . . . . מֵעַם, מֵעָם

from . . . . מֵעִם

To find a word:
- Disregard וְ, וּ, וַ, וָ, וֶ or וִ, (meaning **and**) at the beginning of a word.
- Disregard the dot in the center of letters.
- Check "The Names of God" which are listed separately beginning on page 75.
- Insert **am, is, are** wherever needed to make sense of a sentence in English.

א ב ג ד ה ו ז ח ט י כ ל מ נ ס ע פ צ ק ר ש ת

command you	מְצַוְּךָ
from a rock, from the rock of	מִצּוּר
his commandments	מִצְוֹתָיו
with his commandments, in his commandments	בְּמִצְוֹתָיו
to his commandments	לְמִצְוֹתָיו
your commandments	מִצְוֹתֶיךָ
in your commandments	בְּמִצְוֹתֶיךָ
to your commandments, for your commandments	לְמִצְוֹתֶיךָ
from your commandments	מִמִּצְוֹתֶיךָ
from Zion	מִצִּיּוֹן
who causes to spring forth	מַצְמִיחַ
the one who causes to spring forth	הַמַּצְמִיחַ
Egypt	מִצְרַיִם, מִצְרָיִם
in Egypt	בְּמִצְרַיִם
from Egypt	מִמִּצְרַיִם
who sanctifies	מְקַדֵּשׁ
those who sanctify	מְקַדְּשֵׁי, מְקָדְשֵׁי
place	מָקוֹם
in the place	בַּמָּקוֹם
in a place	בְּמָקוֹם
the place	הַמָּקוֹם
the place, to the place	לַמָּקוֹם

from your people	מֵעַמְּךָ, מֵעַמֶּךָ
from the dust	מֵעָפָר
from evening	מֵעֶרֶב
the doing of, the work of	מַעֲשֵׂה
with the doing of, with the work of	בְּמַעֲשֵׂה
to the doing of, for the doing of, to the work of, for the work of	לְמַעֲשֵׂה
deed	מַעֲשֶׂה
the deed, creation	הַמַּעֲשֶׂה
your works	מַעֲשֶׂיךָ
in your works	בְּמַעֲשֶׂיךָ
as your works	כְּמַעֲשֶׂיךָ
deeds	מַעֲשִׂים
from now	מֵעַתָּה
from my mouth, from the mouth of	מִפִּי
from our mouths	מִפִּינוּ
from the face of, because of	מִפְּנֵי
from before him	מִפָּנָיו
from before you	מִפָּנֶיךָ
Matzo, unleavened Passover bread	מַצָּה

To find a word:

- Disregard וְ, וּ, וַ, וָ, וֶ or וִ, (meaning **and**) at the beginning of a word.
- Disregard the dot in the center of letters.
- Check "The Names of God" which are listed separately beginning on page 75.
- Insert **am, is, are** wherever needed to make sense of a sentence in English.

א ב ג ד ה ו ז ח ט י כ ל מ נ ס ע פ צ ק ר ש ת

- from his name . . . מִשְּׁמוֹ
- (they) make heard . . . מַשְׁמִיעִים
- judgement, justice, the justice of . . . מִשְׁפַּט
  - in judgement, justice . . . בַּמִּשְׁפָּט
  - in judgement, justice . . . בְּמִשְׁפָּט
  - the judgement . . . הַמִּשְׁפָּט
  - for justice, with justice . . . לְמִשְׁפָּט
- the judgement of . . . מִשְׁפַּט
- his serving ones, his ministering angels . . . מְשָׁרְתָיו
- bow . . . מִשְׁתַּחֲוִים
- enemy . . . מַשְׂטִין
- from your Torah . . . מִתּוֹרָתְךָ, מִתּוֹרָתֶךָ
- underneath . . . מִתָּחַת
- dead, the dead . . . מֵתִים
  - the dead . . . הַמֵּתִים
- set free, (one) who sets free . . . מַתִּיר
  - the one who sets free . . . הַמַּתִּיר
- (they) lift themselves up . . . מִתְנַשְּׂאִים

- the place of . . . מְקוֹם
  - in the the place of . . . בִּמְקוֹם
- keep, (one) who keeps . . . מְקַיֵּם
  - the one who keeps . . . הַמְקַיֵּם
- holy festival, holy gathering *(Idiom)* . . . מִקְרָא קֹדֶשׁ
- holy gatherings, holy festivals *(Idiom)* . . . מִקְרָאֵי קֹדֶשׁ
- from the beginning, from the head of . . . מֵרֹאשׁ
- on high . . . מָרוֹם
  - on high . . . בַּמָּרוֹם
  - on high . . . לַמָּרוֹם
  - from on high . . . מִמָּרוֹם
- high places . . . מְרוֹמִים
- bitter (herbs) . . . מָרוֹר
- from evil . . . מֵרָע
- from the wicked ones . . . מֵרְשָׁעִים
- Moses . . . מֹשֶׁה
  - with Moses . . . בְּמֹשֶׁה
  - as Moses . . . כְּמֹשֶׁה
  - to Moses, for Moses . . . לְמֹשֶׁה
- from the song of . . . מִשִּׁיר

To find a word:

- Disregard וְ, וּ, וַ, וָ, וֶ or וִ, (meaning **and**) at the beginning of a word.
- Disregard the dot in the center of letters.
- Check "The Names of God" which are listed separately beginning on page 75.
- Insert **am, is, are** wherever needed to make sense of a sentence in English.

נ

א ב ג ד ה ו ז ח ט י כ ל מ **נ** ס ע פ צ ק ר ש ת

נ

please	נָא
glorious	נֶאְדָּר
faithful	נֶאֱמָן
faithful, the faithful	הַנֶּאֱמָן
it was said	נֶאֱמַר
as it was said	שֶׁנֶּאֱמַר
your prophet	נְבִיאֶךָ
was created	נִבְרָא
we will tell	נַגִּיד
we will thank	נוֹדֶה
stretches out, (one) who stretches out	נוֹטֶה
the fallen	נוֹפְלִים, נֹפְלִים
the fallen	הַנּוֹפְלִים
awesome	נוֹרָא
the awesome one	הַנּוֹרָא
revered in praises, awesome in splendor *(Idiom)*	נוֹרָא תְהִלּוֹת
give, (one) who gives	נוֹתֵן, נֹתֵן
the one who gives	הַנּוֹתֵן
consolation	*(Aramaic)* נֶחֱמָתָא
(he) planted	נָטַע
my banner, my miracle	נִסִּי
miracles	נִסִּים
pleasantness	נֹעַם
may we adore you	נַעֲרִיצְךָ
was made	נַעֲשָׂה
your wonders	נִפְלְאוֹתֶיךָ, נִפְלְאֹתֶיךָ
the fallen	נֹפְלִים, נוֹפְלִים
my soul	נַפְשִׁי
to my soul, for my soul	לְנַפְשִׁי
your soul	נַפְשְׁךָ
and ever	נְצָחִים
forever and ever *(Idiom)*	לְנֵצַח נְצָחִים
let us welcome	נְקַבְּלָה
may we make holy	נַקְדִּישׁ
may we make you holy	נַקְדִּישְׁךָ
we will make holy, let us make holy	נְקַדֵּשׁ
we will hope	נְקַוֶּה

To find a word:

- Disregard וְ, וּ, וַ, וָ, וֶ or וֵ, (meaning **and**) at the beginning of a word.
- Disregard the dot in the center of letters.
- Check "The Names of God" which are listed separately beginning on page 75.
- Insert **am, is, are** wherever needed to make sense of a sentence in English.

נ·ס·ע

was called . . . . נִקְרָא

light, the light of, candle(s), the candle(s) of . . . . נֵר

eternal light *(Idiom)* . . . . נֵר תָּמִיד

let us return . . . . נָשׁוּבָה

my soul . . . . נִשְׁמָתִי

is different . . . . נִשְׁתַּנָּה

her paths, its paths . . . . נְתִיבוֹתֶיהָ

(he) gave . . . . נָתַן

- that (he) gave . . . . שֶׁנָּתַן

give, (one) who gives . . . . . . נֹתֵן, נוֹתֵן

you gave . . . . נָתַתָּ

- that you gave . . . . שֶׁנָּתַתָּ

ס

with your permission *(Aramaic Idiom)* . . . . . סָבְרֵי מָרָנָן

Siddur, prayerbook . . . . סִדּוּר

Seder, Passover meal . . . . סֵדֶר

supports, (one) who supports . . . . . . סוֹמֵךְ

- the one who supports . . . . . . הַסּוֹמֵךְ

Succah, temporary structure for the harvest festival . . . . . . סֻכָּה

Succot, harvest festival symbolized by the Succah . . . . סֻכּוֹת

Selah (uncertain meaning) . . . . סֶלָה

Forgive! . . . . סְלַח

forgiveness; Selichot, service on Saturday night before Rosh Hashona . . סְלִיחוֹת

book, the book of . . . . סֵפֶר

- in the book . . . . בַּסֵּפֶר
- in the book of . . . . בְּסֵפֶר

ע

your servant . . . . עַבְדְּךָ, עַבְדֶּךָ

- to your servant, for your servant . . . . לְעַבְדְּךָ, לְעַבְדֶּךָ

until . . . . עַד

again, yet, another, any more . . . . עוֹד

help, (one) who helps . . . . עוֹזֵר

our children . . . . עוֹלָלֵינוּ

To find a word:

- Disregard וְ, וּ, וַ, וָ, וֶ or וֵ, (meaning **and**) at the beginning of a word.
- Disregard the dot in the center of letters.
- Check "The Names of God" which are listed separately beginning on page 75.
- Insert **am, is, are** wherever needed to make sense of a sentence in English.

א ב ג ד ה ו ז ח ט י כ ל מ נ ס ע פ צ ק ר ש ת

עוֹלָם — eternity, universe
- בָּעוֹלָם — in eternity, in the world
- הָעוֹלָם — eternity, the universe
- לְעוֹלָם, לְעֹלָם — forever
- מֵעוֹלָם — from the earliest time
- לְעוֹלָם וָעֶד — forever and ever *(Idiom)*

עוֹלָמִים, עֹלָמִים — eternity, universe
- הָעוֹלָמִים — eternity, the universe
- לְעוֹלָמִים — forever

עוֹמֵד — stand, (one) who stands

עוֹשֵׂה, עֹשֵׂה — the doer of, the maker of
- לְעוֹשֵׂה — to the doer of, to the maker of

עוֹשֶׂה, עֹשֶׂה — do, (one) who does, make, (one) who makes
- הָעוֹשֶׂה — the one who does, the one who makes

עֹז, עוֹז — strength, the strength of
- בְּעוֹז — with strength, with the strength of
- הָעֹז — the strength

עֻזּוֹ — his strength

עֻזְּךָ — your strength

עֵינֵי — the eyes of
- בְּעֵינֵי — in the eyes of
- לְעֵינֵי — before the eyes of

עֵינֶיךָ — your eyes
- בְּעֵינֶיךָ — in your eyes

עֵינֵינוּ — our eyes
- בְּעֵינֵינוּ — in our eyes
- לְעֵינֵינוּ — before our eyes

עִיר — city, the city of
- בָּעִיר — in the city
- בְּעִיר — in the city, in the city of

עַל — on, about, near
- מֵעַל — above
- שֶׁעַל — that is on, that are on

עַל חֵטְא — for the sin *(Idiom)*

עַל יַד — near, by the hand of *(Idiom)*

עַל כֵּן — therefore *(Idiom)*

עַל פִּי — according to *(Idiom)*

עֹל — yoke, the yoke of

עָלַי — on me, about me, against me
- מֵעָלַי — from me, against me

עֲלֵיהֶם — on them, for them

עֶלְיוֹן — the highest
- הָעֶלְיוֹן — the highest

To find a word:
- Disregard וְ, וּ, וַ, וָ, וֶ or וִ, (meaning **and**) at the beginning of a word.
- Disregard the dot in the center of letters.
- Check "The Names of God" which are listed separately beginning on page 75.
- Insert **am, is, are** wherever needed to make sense of a sentence in English.

א ב ג ד ה ו ז ח ט י כ ל מ נ ס ע פ צ ק ר ש ת

on you . . . . עֲלֵיכֶם

on us, it is upon us . . . . עָלֵינוּ
- from upon us . . . . מֵעָלֵינוּ

forever . . . . *(Aramaic)* עָלְמַיָּא
- forever and ever *(Aramaic Idiom)* . . לְעָלַם וּלְעָלְמֵי עָלְמַיָּא

eternity, universe . . . עֹלָמִים, עוֹלָמִים

people, nation, the people of . . . . עַם, עָם
- against the people, among the people, the people . . . . בָּעָם
- with a people . . . . בְּעַם
- the people . . . . הָעָם
- to the people . . . . לָעָם
- as a people, to a people, as the people of, to the people of . . לְעָם, לְעַם
- from a people, from the people, from the people of . . . . מֵעַם, מֵעָם

with . . . . עִם
- from . . . . מֵעִם

his people . . . . עַמּוֹ
- in his people, with his people . . . בְּעַמּוֹ
- to his people . . . . לְעַמּוֹ

peoples, the peoples . . . . עַמִּים
- among the peoples . . . . בָּעַמִּים
- the peoples . . . . הָעַמִּים

your people . . . . עַמְּךָ, עַמֶּךָ
- on your people . . . . . בְּעַמְּךָ, בְּעַמֶּךָ
- like your people . . . . . כְּעַמְּךָ, כְּעַמֶּךָ
- to your people, your people . לְעַמְּךָ, לְעַמֶּךָ
- from your people . . . . מֵעַמְּךָ, מֵעַמֶּךָ

with us . . . . עִמָּנוּ

Omer, an ancient grain measure, the days counted between Passover and Shavuot . . עֹמֶר
- the Omer . . . . הָעֹמֶר
- of the Omer . . . . לָעֹמֶר

(they) answered . . . . עָנוּ

answer us . . . . עֲנֵנוּ

dust . . . . עָפָר
- in the dust . . . . בֶּעָפָר
- the dust . . . . הֶעָפָר
- as dust . . . . כֶּעָפָר
- to the dust . . . . לֶעָפָר
- as dust . . . . לְעָפָר
- from the dust . . . . מֵעָפָר

tree . . . . עֵץ

a tree of life *(Idiom)* . . . . עֵץ חַיִּים

evening . . . . עֶרֶב
- in the evening . . . . בָּעֶרֶב
- in the evening of . . . . בְּעֶרֶב
- from evening . . . . מֵעֶרֶב

To find a word:
- Disregard וְ, וּ, וַ, וָ, וֶ or וֵ, (meaning **and**) at the beginning of a word.
- Disregard the dot in the center of letters.
- Check "The Names of God" which are listed separately beginning on page 75.
- Insert **am, is, are** wherever needed to make sense of a sentence in English.

(he) did, (he) made . . . . עָשָׂה
- who did, who made . . . . שֶׁעָשָׂה

do, (one) who does, make, (one) who makes . . . . . עֹשֶׂה, עוֹשֶׂה
- the one who does, the one who makes . . . . הָעֹשֶׂה
- to the one who does, to the one who makes . . . . לְעֹשֶׂה

the doer of, the maker of . . עֹשֵׂה, עוֹשֵׂה
- to the doer of, to the maker of . לְעוֹשֵׂה

Do! Make! . . . . עֲשֵׂה

you did, you made . . . . עָשִׂיתָ
- that you did, that you made . . . שֶׁעָשִׂיתָ

(who) made us . . . . עָשָׂנוּ

time, time of, season, season of . . . . . עֵת
- in the season, in the time . . . . . . בָּעֵת
- at the time of, in the season of . . . בְּעֵת
- at the time of . . . . לְעֵת

now . . . . עַתָּה, עָתָּה
- from now . . . . מֵעַתָּה

פ

Redeem! Save! . . . . פְּדֵה

Purim, festival celebrating the story of Esther . . . . פּוּרִים

my mouth, the mouth of . . . . פִּי
- in my mouth, in the mouth of . . . . בְּפִי
- as my mouth, as the mouth of, according to . . . כְּפִי
- at my mouth, at the mouth of, according to . . . . לְפִי
- from my mouth, from the mouth of . . . . מִפִּי
- according to *(Idiom)* . . . . עַל פִּי

wonders . . . . פֶּלֶא

the face of . . . . פְּנֵי
- in the face of, in front of . . . . . . בִּפְנֵי
- before, in front of . . . . לִפְנֵי
- from the face of, because of . . . . . מִפְּנֵי

his face . . . . פָּנָיו
- before him . . . . לְפָנָיו
- from before him . . . . מִפָּנָיו

your face . . . . פָּנֶיךָ
- before you, in front of you . . . . לְפָנֶיךָ
- from before you . . . . מִפָּנֶיךָ

To find a word:
- Disregard וְ, וּ, וַ, וָ, וֶ or וִ, (meaning **and**) at the beginning of a word.
- Disregard the dot in the center of letters.
- Check "The Names of God" which are listed separately beginning on page 75.
- Insert **am, is, are** wherever needed to make sense of a sentence in English.

פ · צ

א ב ג ד ה ו ז ח ט י כ ל מ נ ס ע פ צ ק ר ש ת

צֶדֶק	righteousness
בְּצֶדֶק	with righteousness
הַצֶּדֶק	the righteousness, righteousness
צְדָקָה	righteousness, charity as righteousness
בִּצְדָקָה	with righteousness
הַצְּדָקָה	the righteousness
לִצְדָקָה	for righteousness
צִוָּנוּ	(he) commanded us
וְצִוָּנוּ	and (he) commanded us
שֶׁצִּוָּנוּ	who commanded us
צוּר	rock, the rock of
הַצּוּר	the rock
לְצוּר	to the rock of
מִצּוּר	from a rock, from the rock of
צוּרִי	my rock
צִיּוֹן	Zion, Jerusalem, the land of Israel
בְּצִיּוֹן	in Zion
לְצִיּוֹן	to Zion
מִצִּיּוֹן	from Zion
צַר	oppressor
צָרָה	trouble, distress
בַּצָּרָה	in trouble, in distress
בְּצָרָה	in trouble, in distress
הַצָּרָה	the trouble, the distress

פֶּסַח	Passover, the festival celebrating the exodus from Egypt
פַּעַם	time, one time
פַּעֲמַיִם	twice
פְּעָמִים	times
פְּרִי	fruit, the fruit of

צ

צֵאתְכֶם	(may) your going out
צְבָאוֹת	multitudes, hosts
צְבָאָם	their multitude
צַדִּיק	righteous, righteous one
הַצַּדִּיק	the righteous one, righteous
לַצַּדִּיק	for the righteous, to the righteous
צַדִּיקִים	righteous, righteous ones
הַצַּדִּיקִים	the righteous, the righteous ones
לַצַּדִּיקִים	for the righteous, to the righteous

To find a word:

- Disregard וְ, וּ, וַ, וָ, וֶ or וֵ, (meaning **and**) at the beginning of a word.
- Disregard the dot in the center of letters.
- Check "The Names of God" which are listed separately beginning on page 75.
- Insert **am, is, are** wherever needed to make sense of a sentence in English.

ת ש ר ק צ פ ע ס נ מ ל כ י ט ח ז ו ה ד ג ב א

ק

- holy, holy one . . . קָדוֹשׁ
  - the holy one . . . הַקָּדוֹשׁ
- the holy one of . . . קְדוֹשׁ
- holy, holy ones . . . קְדוֹשִׁים, קְדֹשִׁים
  - the holy ones . . . הַקְּדוֹשִׁים
- holiness, the holiness of, holy place . . . קֹדֶשׁ
  - in holiness, in the holy place . . . בְּקֹדֶשׁ
  - holiness, the holy place . . . הַקֹּדֶשׁ
  - for the holy place . . . לְקֹדֶשׁ
  - holy gathering, holy festival *(Idiom)* . . . מִקְרָא קֹדֶשׁ
  - holy gatherings, holy festivals *(Idiom)* . . . מִקְרָאֵי קֹדֶשׁ
- the holy of holies *(Idiom)* . . . קֹדֶשׁ הַקֳּדָשִׁים
- his holiness, his holy place . . . קָדְשׁוֹ
  - in his holiness, in his holy place . . . בְּקָדְשׁוֹ
  - his holy place, to his holy pace . . . לְקָדְשׁוֹ
- your holiness, your holy place . . . קָדְשְׁךָ, קָדְשֶׁךָ
  - for your holy name *(Idiom)* . . . לְשֵׁם קָדְשֶׁךָ
- (who) made us holy . . . קִדְּשָׁנוּ
- you have made holy . . . קִדַּשְׁתָּ
- your holiness . . . קְדֻשָּׁתְךָ, קְדֻשָּׁתֶךָ
- voice, the voice of . . . קוֹל, קֹל
  - with a voice, with the voice of . . . בְּקוֹל
  - to the voice of . . . לְקוֹל
- our voice . . . קוֹלֵנוּ
- Arise! . . . קוּמָה
- (one) who is master of . . . קוֹנֵה, קֹנֵה
- enduring . . . קַיָּם
- (who) preserved us . . . קִיְּמָנוּ
- voice, the voice of . . . קֹל, קוֹל
- (he) called . . . קָרָא
- near . . . קָרוֹב
  - soon . . . בְּקָרוֹב
  - to the near one, to the near . . . לַקָּרוֹב
- soon . . . *(Aramaic)* קָרִיב
- strength, the strength of, horn . . . קֶרֶן
- you bound them . . . קְשַׁרְתָּם
  - may you bind them, you shall bind them . . . וּקְשַׁרְתָּם

To find a word:

- Disregard וְ, וּ, וַ, וָ, וֶ or וִ, (meaning **and**) at the beginning of a word.
- Disregard the dot in the center of letters.
- Check "The Names of God" which are listed separately beginning on page 75.
- Insert **am, is, are** wherever needed to make sense of a sentence in English.

ר

א ב ג ד ה ו ז ח ט י כ ל מ נ ס ע פ צ ק ר ש ת

(they) saw . . . . רָאוּ

head, the head of, beginning, the beginning of . . . . . . רֹאשׁ

as a head, as the head of . . . . . לְרֹאשׁ

from the beginning, from the head of . . . . מֵרֹאשׁ

Rosh Hashanah, New Year . . רֹאשׁ הַשָּׁנָה

on Rosh Hashanah . . . . בְּרֹאשׁ הַשָּׁנָה

beginning . . . . רֵאשִׁית

many, much, numerous . . . . רַב, רָב

numerous . . . . הָרָב

great . . . . *(Aramaic)* רַבָּא

much, many, lots of . . . . רַבָּה

Rabbi, my teacher . . . . רַבִּי

many, much . . . . רַבִּים

the many, many . . . . הָרַבִּים

Rebecca . . . . רִבְקָה

spirit, the spirit of, breath, the breath of . רוּחַ

by the spirit of, by the breath of . בְּרוּחַ

the spirit, the breath . . . . הָרוּחַ

my spirit . . . . רוּחִי

cure, (one) who cures . . . . . רוֹפֵא, רֹפֵא

the one who cures . . . . הָרוֹפֵא

compassionate . . . . רַחוּם

Rachael . . . . רָחֵל

Have compassion! . . . . רַחֵם

as (one) has compassion . . . . . . כְּרַחֵם

to have compassion . . . . לְרַחֵם

your compassion . . . . רַחֲמֶיךָ

with your compassion . . . . . בְּרַחֲמֶיךָ

compassion . . . . רַחֲמִים

with compassion . . . . בְּרַחֲמִים

the compassion . . . . הָרַחֲמִים

compassion, for compassion . . לְרַחֲמִים

compassionate . . . . רַחֲמָן

the compassionate one . . . . . הָרַחֲמָן

joy, joyous song . . . . רִנָּה

with joy, with joyous song . . . . . בְּרִנָּה

evil . . . . רָע

the evil, evil . . . . הָרָע

evil, for evil . . . . לָרָע

from evil . . . . מֵרָע

To find a word:

- Disregard וְ, וּ, וַ, וָ, וֶ or וִ, (meaning **and**) at the beginning of a word.
- Disregard the dot in the center of letters.
- Check "The Names of God" which are listed separately beginning on page 75.
- Insert **am, is, are** wherever needed to make sense of a sentence in English.

א ב ג ד ה ו ז ח ט י כ ל מ נ ס ע פ צ ק ר ש ת

famine . . . . רָעָב

evil . . . . רָעָה
- the evil, evil . . . . הָרָעָה
- for evil, evil . . . . לְרָעָה

loud . . . . רַעַשׁ

cure, (one) who cures . . . . . רֹפֵא, רוֹפֵא

(he) was pleased . . . . רָצָה

Be pleased with! Accept! . . . . רְצֵה

will, good will, favor . . . . רָצוֹן
- with favor . . . . בְּרָצוֹן
- favorable . . . . לְרָצוֹן

your will . . . . רְצוֹנְךָ, רְצוֹנֶךָ
- according to your will בִּרְצוֹנְךָ, בִּרְצוֹנֶךָ

the wicked of . . . . רִשְׁעֵי

wicked ones . . . . רְשָׁעִים
- the wicked ones . . . . הָרְשָׁעִים
- for the wicked ones . . . . . . לָרְשָׁעִים
- from the wicked ones . . . . . מֵרְשָׁעִים

שׁ

who, which, that . . . . שֶׁ
(always attached to the beginning of a word)

when man . . . . שֶׁאָדָם

that love . . . . שֶׁאָהֲבָה

that you have loved . . . . שֶׁאָהַבְתָּ

who is without . . . . שֶׁאֵין

that if . . . . שֶׁאִם

that (he) said . . . . שֶׁאָמַר

that we . . . . שֶׁאֲנַחְנוּ

that I . . . . שֶׁאֲנִי

the rest of . . . . שְׁאָר

that comes . . . . שֶׁבָּא

Shavuot, festival celebrating the giving of the Torah . . . שָׁבוּעוֹת

(they) praised . . . . שִׁבְּחוּ

your praise . . . . שִׁבְחֲךָ

that is between . . . . שֶׁבֵּין

To find a word:
- Disregard וְ, וּ, וַ, וָ, וֶ or וֵ, (meaning **and**) at the beginning of a word.
- Disregard the dot in the center of letters.
- Check "The Names of God" which are listed separately beginning on page 75.
- Insert **am, is, are** wherever needed to make sense of a sentence in English.

א ב ג ד ה ו ז ח ט י כ ל מ נ ס ע פ צ ק ר ש ת

שְׁבִיעִי	seventh
בַּשְּׁבִיעִי	on the seventh
הַשְּׁבִיעִי	the seventh
שֶׁבְּכָל	that on all of, that with all of
שֶׁבַּשָּׁמַיִם	that in the heavens
שָׁבַת	(he) ceased working, (he) rested
שַׁבָּת	Shabbat, Sabbath
בַּשַּׁבָּת	on the Sabbath
הַשַּׁבָּת	the Sabbath
לַשַּׁבָּת	the Sabbath, for the Sabbath
שַׁבַּת	the Sabbath of
שֶׁהַבּוֹרֵא	that the one who creates
שֶׁהוּא	that he, that it
שֶׁהֶחֱזַרְתָּ	that you have returned
שֶׁהֶחֱיָנוּ	who has made us live
שֶׁהִיא	that it
שֶׁהָיָה	who was, that was
שֶׁהָיוּ	who were, that were
שֶׁהַכֹּל	that all
שֶׁהַמֶּלֶךְ	that the king
שֶׁהַשִּׂמְחָה	that the joy
שׁוֹאֲלִים	(they) ask
שׁוֹמֵר, שֹׁמֵר	keep, (one) who keeps guard, (one) who guards
הַשּׁוֹמֵר	the one who keeps, the one who guards
שׁוֹפָר	Shofar, ram's horn, used in high holiday prayers
שֶׁחָטָאנוּ	that we have sinned
שֶׁיָּבֹא	that will come
שֶׁיִּהְיוּ	that (they) will be
שֶׁיַּעֲשֶׂה	that (he) will make, that (he) will do
שִׁיר	song, the song of
בְּשִׁיר	with song
הַשִּׁיר	the song
מִשִּׁיר	from the song of
שִׁירָה	a song
שִׁירָתָא (Aramaic)	songs
שֶׁכֻּלָּם	that all of them
שֶׁל	of
שֶׁלֹּא	that not, who not

To find a word:

- Disregard וְ, וּ, וַ, וָ, וֶ or וִ, (meaning **and**) at the beginning of a word.
- Disregard the dot in the center of letters.
- Check "The Names of God" which are listed separately beginning on page 75.
- Insert **am, is, are** wherever needed to make sense of a sentence in English.

א ב ג ד ה ו ז ח ט י כ ל מ נ ס ע פ צ ק ר ש ת

his name (usually referring to God) . . שְׁמוֹ
- in his name . . . . בִּשְׁמוֹ
- as his name . . . . כִּשְׁמוֹ
- to his name . . . . לִשְׁמוֹ
- from his name . . . . מִשְּׁמוֹ

Guard! Keep! . . . . שְׁמוֹר, שְׁמֹר

the heavens . . . . (Aramaic) שְׁמַיָּא
- in heaven . . . . (Aramaic) בִּשְׁמַיָּא

the heavens . . . . שָׁמַיִם, שָׁמָיִם
- in the heavens . . . . בַּשָּׁמַיִם
- the heavens . . . . הַשָּׁמַיִם
- to the heavens . . . . לַשָּׁמַיִם
- that in the heavens . . . . . . שֶׁבַּשָּׁמַיִם

your name . . . . שִׁמְךָ, שְׁמֶךָ
(usually referring to God)
- in your name . . . . . . בִּשְׁמְךָ, בִּשְׁמֶךָ
- as your name . . . . . . כְּשִׁמְךָ, כִּשְׁמֶךָ
- to your name . . . . . . לְשִׁמְךָ, לִשְׁמֶךָ

that is from him, ... שֶׁמִּמֶּנּוּ
that is from it,
that is from us

Hear! Listen! . . . . שְׁמַע

as (they) make holy . . . . . . שֶׁמַּקְדִּישִׁים

keep, (one) who keeps, . . . שֹׁמֵר, שׁוֹמֵר
guard, (one) who guards

peace, inner peace, completeness . . שָׁלוֹם
- with peace . . . . בַּשָּׁלוֹם
- with peace . . . . בְּשָׁלוֹם
- the peace, peace . . . . הַשָּׁלוֹם
- for peace, in peace . . . . לְשָׁלוֹם

your (God's) peace . . . . שְׁלוֹמֶךָ
- with your (God's) peace . . . . בִּשְׁלוֹמֶךָ

yours . . . . שֶׁלָּךְ

yours . . . . שֶׁלְּךָ

complete, perfect . . . . שָׁלֵם, שַׁלֵּם
- to complete . . . . לְשַׁלֵּם

peace, inner peace . . . . . (Aramaic) שְׁלָמָא

complete, perfect . . . . שְׁלֵמָה

there . . . . שָׁם
- that there . . . . שֶׁשָּׁם

name, the name of . . . . שֵׁם
- in the name of, by name . . . . . . בְּשֵׁם
- the name, ... הַשֵּׁם
  a way of referring to God
- as the name of, ... כְּשֵׁם
  just as the name
- in the name of, for renown . . . . . לְשֵׁם

his name (God's) . . . . (Aramaic) שְׁמֵהּ

To find a word:
- Disregard וְ, וּ, וַ, וָ, וֶ or וִ, (meaning **and**) at the beginning of a word.
- Disregard the dot in the center of letters.
- Check "The Names of God" which are listed separately beginning on page 75.
- Insert **am, is, are** wherever needed to make sense of a sentence in English.

א ב ג ד ה ו ז ח ט י כ ל מ נ ס ע פ צ ק ר ש ש ת

that you did, that you made . . . . . שֶׁעָשִׂיתָ

who commanded us . . . . שֶׁצִּוָּנוּ

serving . . . . שָׁרֵת

that there . . . . שֶׁשָּׁם

six . . . . שֵׁשֶׁת

two . . . . שְׁתֵּי

saying of . . . . שִׂיחַ

Put! . . . . שִׂים

(he) put . . . . שָׂם

joy, delight . . . . שִׂמְחָה

- with joy, with delight . . . . . . בְּשִׂמְחָה
- for joy, with delight . . . . לְשִׂמְחָה
- that the joy . . . . שֶׁהַשִּׂמְחָה

Simchat Torah, festival celebrating the ending and the beginning of the reading of the Torah . . . שִׂמְחַת תּוֹרָה

put us . . . . שָׂמָנוּ

(they) kept, (they) guarded . . . . . . שָׁמְרוּ

- may (they) keep, (they) shall keep . וְשָׁמְרוּ

as it was said . . . . שֶׁנֶּאֱמַר

year . . . . שָׁנָה

- in the year . . . . בַּשָּׁנָה
- the year . . . . הַשָּׁנָה
- to the year . . . . לַשָּׁנָה
- for a good year, Happy New Year *(Idiom)* . . . . . . לְשָׁנָה טוֹבָה
- next year in Jerusalem *(Idiom)* . . לְשָׁנָה הַבָּאָה בִּירוּשָׁלַיִם

second . . . . שֵׁנִי

a second time . . . . שֵׁנִית

you taught them . . . . שִׁנַּנְתָּם

- may you teach them, you shall teach them . . . . . וְשִׁנַּנְתָּם

that (he) gave . . . . שֶׁנָּתַן

that you gave . . . . שֶׁנָּתַתָּ

hour . . . . שָׁעָה

that is on, that are on . . . . שֶׁעַל

the gates of . . . . שַׁעֲרֵי

who did, who made . . . . שֶׁעָשָׂה

To find a word:

- Disregard וְ, וּ, וַ, וָ, וֶ or וִ, (meaning **and**) at the beginning of a word.
- Disregard the dot in the center of letters.
- Check "The Names of God" which are listed separately beginning on page 75.
- Insert **am, is, are** wherever needed to make sense of a sentence in English.

lips of, edge of . . . שְׂפַת

my lips . . . שְׂפָתַי

Sarah . . . שָׂרָה

Seraphim of . . . שַׂרְפֵי

the Seraphim . . . שְׂרָפִים

joy, delight . . . שָׂשׂוֹן
- with joy . . . בְּשָׂשׂוֹן
- for joy, for delight . . . לְשָׂשׂוֹן

ת

world, earth . . . תֵּבֵל
- in the world . . . בְּתֵבֵל

you will be . . . תְּהִי

praise . . . תְּהִלָּה
- with praise . . . בִּתְהִלָּה
- for praise . . . לִתְהִלָּה

praises, praises of . . . תְּהִלּוֹת, תְּהִלֹּת
- revered in praises, awesome in splendor *(Idiom)* . . . נוֹרָא תְהִלּוֹת

your praise . . . תְּהִלָּתֶךָ
- in your praise . . . בִּתְהִלָּתֶךָ

its supporters . . . תּוֹמְכֶיהָ

Torah, law, the first five books of the Bible . . . תּוֹרָה
- in the Torah . . . בַּתּוֹרָה
- the Torah . . . הַתּוֹרָה
- according to the law, according to the Torah . . . כַּתּוֹרָה
- to the Torah . . . לַתּוֹרָה

the Torah of, the law of . . . תּוֹרַת
- in the Torah of, in the law of . . . בְּתוֹרַת

his Torah . . . תּוֹרָתוֹ
- in his Torah . . . בְּתוֹרָתוֹ

your Torah . . . תּוֹרָתְךָ, תּוֹרָתֶךָ
- in your Torah . . . בְּתוֹרָתְךָ, בְּתוֹרָתֶךָ
- for your Torah . . . לְתוֹרָתְךָ, לְתוֹרָתֶךָ
- from your Torah . . . מִתּוֹרָתְךָ, מִתּוֹרָתֶךָ

beginning . . . תְּחִלָּה

end . . . תַּכְלִית

will bend . . . תִּכְרַע

continually . . . תָּמִיד
- continually . . . לְתָמִיד
- eternal light *(Idiom)* . . . נֵר תָּמִיד

you will rule . . . תִּמְלוֹךְ

Give! . . . תֵּן, תֶּן

To find a word:
- Disregard וְ, וּ, וַ, וָ, וֶ or וִ, (meaning **and**) at the beginning of a word.
- Disregard the dot in the center of letters.
- Check "The Names of God" which are listed separately beginning on page 75.
- Insert **am, is, are** wherever needed to make sense of a sentence in English.

א	ב	ג	ד	ה	ו	ז	ח	ט	י	כ	ל	מ	נ	ס	ע	פ	צ	ק	ר	ש	ת

glory, the glory of . . . . תִּפְאֶרֶת

- with glory, with the glory of . . בְּתִפְאֶרֶת
- the glory . . . . הַתִּפְאֶרֶת
- for glory, for the glory of . . . לְתִפְאֶרֶת

prayer . . . . תְּפִלָּה

Tefillin, leather box used in prayer containing quotations from the Bible . תְּפִילִּין

their prayer . . . . תְּפִלָּתָם

may you open, you shall open . תִּפְתָּח, תִּפְתַּח

the first word for sounding the Shofar . . . . תְּקִיעָה

praises . . . . *(Aramaic)* תֻּשְׁבְּחָתָא

(you) will swear . . . . תִּשָּׁבַע

To find a word:

- Disregard וְ, וּ, וַ, וָ, וֶ or וִ, (meaning **and**) at the beginning of a word.
- Disregard the dot in the center of letters.
- Check "The Names of God" which are listed separately beginning on page 75.
- Insert **am, is, are** wherever needed to make sense of a sentence in English.

Key to Pronunciation Guide

Consonants

B as in **B**oy	בּ
CH as in Ba**CH**	ח כ ך
D as in **D**oor	ד
F as in **F**ood	פ ף
G as in **G**irl	ג
H as in **H**ouse	ה
K as in **K**itty	כּ ק
L as in **L**ook	ל
M as in **M**other	מ ם
N as in **N**ow	נ ן
P as in **P**eople	פּ
R as in **R**obin	ר
S as in **S**un	ס שׂ
SH as in **SH**ape	שׁ
T as in **T**all	ט ת
TS as in nu**TS**	צ ץ
V as in **V**ine	ב ו
Y as in **Y**es	י
Z as in **Z**ebra	ז

Vowels

Sound	Vowels
a as in y**a**cht	Xַ Xָ
ee as in b**ee**	Xִי Xִ
ay as in h**ay**	Xֵי Xֵ
e as in b**e**d	Xֶ
o as in l**o**w	Xוֹ Xֹ
oo as in z**oo**	Xוּ Xֻ
ai as in **ai**sle	Xַי
oi as in b**oi**l	Xוֹי
silent	Xְ

א · ב

א ב ג ד ה ו ז ח ט י כ ל מ נ ס ע פ צ ק ר ש ת

א

אָב, אַב	**av**
אָבוֹת, אָבֹת	a-**vot**
אֲבוֹתֵינוּ, אֲבֹתֵינוּ	a-vo-**tay**-noo
אָבִינוּ	a-**vee**-noo
אַבְרָהָם	av-ra-**ham**
אָדוֹן	a-**don**
אֲדוֹן	a-**don**
אַדִּיר	a-**deer**
אַדִּירֵנוּ	a-dee-**ray**-noo
אָדָם	a-**dam**
אֲדָמָה	a-da-**ma**
אַהֲבָה	a-ha-**va**
אָהַבְתָּ	a-**hav**-ta
אַהֲבַת	a-ha-**vat**
אוֹכְלִין	och-**leen**
אוֹמֵר, אֹמֵר	o-**mayr**
אוֹמְרִים	om-**reem**
אוֹר	**or**
אוֹת	**ot**
אוֹתוֹ, אֹתוֹ	o-**to**
אוֹתָנוּ	o-**ta**-noo
אָז	**az**
אֲזַי	a-**zai**
אֶחָד	e-**chad**
אַחַד	a-**chad**
אַחֲרֵי	a-cha-**ray**
אַחַת	a-**chat**
אֶחָת	e-**chat**
אַיֵּה	a-**yay**
אֵין	**ayn**
אִירָא	ee-**ra**
אִישׁ	**eesh**
אִישָׁן	ee-**shan**
אַל	**al**
אֵל	**el**
אֶלָּא	**e**-la
אֵלֶּה	**ay**-le
אֵלֶיךָ	ay-**le**-cha
אֱלִילִים	e-lee-**leem**
אִם	**eem**
אֱמוּנָה	e-moo-**na**
אֱמוּנָתוֹ	e-moo-na-**to**
אֱמוּנָתֶךָ	e-moo-na-**te**-cha
אָמֵן	a-**mayn**
אָמַר	a-**mar**
אֹמֵר, אוֹמֵר	o-**mayr**
אָמְרוּ	am-**roo**
אִמְרוּ	eem-**roo**
אִמְרֵי	eem-**ray**
אֱמֶת	e-**met**
אָנוּ	**a**-noo
אֲנַחְנוּ	a-**nach**-noo
אֲנִי, אָנִי	a-**nee**
אָנֹכִי	a-**no**-chee
אֲסוּרִים	a-soo-**reem**
אָעִירָה	a-ee-**ra**
אַף	**af**
אֲפִילוּ	a-**fee**-loo
אֶפֶס	**e**-fes
אַפְקִיד	af-**keed**
אֶקְרָא	**ek**-ra
אֲרוֹן הַקֹּדֶשׁ	a-**ron** ha-**ko**-desh
אֶרֶץ	**e**-rets
אָרֶץ	**a**-rets
אֵשׁ	**aysh**
אֲשֶׁר	a-**sher**
אַשְׁרֵי	ash-**ray**
אֶת	**et**
אֵת	**ayt**
אַתָּה	a-**ta**
אֶתְכֶם	et-**chem**
אֶתְרוֹג	et-**rog**

ב

בְּ	**b**
בַּ, בָּ	**ba**
בֶּ	**be**
בִּ	**bee**
בָּא	**ba**
בָּאָדָם	ba-a-**dam**
בְּאַהֲבָה	ba-a-ha-**va**
בְּאוֹר	b-**or**
בְּאֶחָד	b-e-**chad**
בְּאֵלֶּה	b-**ay**-le
בֶּאֱמוּנָה	be-e-moo-**na**
בֶּאֱמוּנָתוֹ	be-e-moo-na-**to**
בְּאִמְרֵי	b-eem-**ray**
בֶּאֱמֶת	be-e-**met**
בְּאַף	b-**af**
בָּאָרֶץ	ba-**a**-rets
בְּאֶרֶץ	b-**e**-rets
בָּאֵשׁ	ba-**aysh**
בַּאֲשֶׁר	ba-a-**sher**
בְּבֵית	b-**vayt**
בְּבֵיתְךָ	b-vayt-**cha**
בְּבֵיתֶךָ	b-vay-**te**-cha
בְּבֵן	b-**ven**
בִּבְנֵי	beev-**nay**
בְּבָנֶיךָ	b-va-**ne**-cha
בְּבַעַל	b-**va**-al
בַּבֹּקֶר	ba-**bo**-ker

ב

bay-**te**-cha	בֵּיתֶךָ
b-cha-**vod**	בְּכָבוֹד
beech-vo-**do**	בִּכְבוֹדוֹ
beech-vo-**de**-cha	בִּכְבוֹדֶךָ
ba-**kol**	בַּכֹּל
b-**chol**	בְּכָל
b-**chayn**	בְּכֵן
b-**lo**	בְּלֹא
b-**layv**	בְּלֵב
b-lay-**vav**	בְּלֵבָב
b-lee-**bee**	בְּלִבִּי
b-lee-**bay**-noo	בְּלִבֵּנוּ
b-**lee**	בְּלִי
ba-**lai**-la	בַּלַּיְלָה
b-**lech**-t-cha	בְּלֶכְתְּךָ
bam	בָּם
ba-**ma**	בַּמָּה
beem-hay-**ra**	בִּמְהֵרָה
ba-**mai**-yeem	בַּמַּיִם
b-**ma**-yeem	בְּמַיִם
b-mal-**choot**	בְּמַלְכוּת
b-mal-choo-**tay**	בְּמַלְכוּתֵהּ
b-mal-choot-**cha**	בְּמַלְכוּתְךָ
b-mal-choo-**te**-cha	בְּמַלְכוּתֶךָ
b-ma-a-**say**	בְּמַעֲשֵׂה
b-ma-a-**se**-cha	בְּמַעֲשֶׂיךָ
b-meets-vo-**tav**	בְּמִצְוֹתָיו
b-meets-vo-**te**-cha	בְּמִצְוֹתֶיךָ
b-meets-**ra**-yeem	בְּמִצְרַיִם
ba-ma-**kom**	בַּמָּקוֹם
b-ma-**kom**	בְּמָקוֹם
beem-**kom**	בִּמְקוֹם
ba-ma-**rom**	בַּמָּרוֹם
beem-ro-**mav**	בִּמְרוֹמָיו
ba-**char**-ta	בָּחַרְתָּ
ba-**cho**-shech	בַּחֹשֶׁךְ
ba-**tov**	בַּטּוֹב
b-**toov**-cha	בְּטוּבְךָ
b-too-**ve**-cha	בְּטוּבֶךָ
b-**te**-rem	בְּטֶרֶם
bee	בִּי
b-**yad**	בְּיַד
b-**yad**	בְּיַד
b-ya-**do**	בְּיָדוֹ
bee-**day**	בִּידֵי
b-yad-**cha**	בְּיָדְךָ
b-ya-**de**-cha	בְּיָדֶךָ
ba-**yom**	בַּיּוֹם
b-**yom**	בְּיוֹם
b-yo-may-**chon**	בְּיוֹמֵיכוֹן
ba-**yam**	בַּיָּם
bee-**ma**	בִּימָה
bee-**may**	בִּימֵי
ba-ya-**meem**	בַּיָּמִים
b-ya-**may**-noo	בְּיָמֵינוּ
bee-meen-**cha**	בִּימִינְךָ
bee-mee-**ne**-cha	בִּימִינֶךָ
bayn	בֵּין
bay-**nee**	בֵּינִי
b-ya-a-**kov**	בְּיַעֲקֹב
b-yeer-**a**	בְּיִרְאָה
bee-roo-sha-**lai**-yeem	בִּירוּשָׁלַיִם
bee-shoo-**a**	בִּישׁוּעָה
bee-shoo-at-**cha**	בִּישׁוּעָתְךָ
bee-shoo-a-**te**-cha	בִּישׁוּעָתֶךָ
b-yees-ra-**ayl**	בְּיִשְׂרָאֵל
bayt	בֵּית
bayt-**cha**	בֵּיתְךָ
b-**gav**-hay	בְּגָבְהֵי
beeg-**voo**-rot	בִּגְבוּרוֹת
ba-**goi**-yeem	בַּגּוֹיִם
ba-da-**var**	בַּדָּבָר
beed-**var**	בִּדְבַר
b-deev-**ray**	בְּדִבְרֵי
b-**dor** va-**dor**	בְּדוֹר וָדוֹר
b-**da**-at	בְּדַעַת
ba-**de**-rech	בַּדֶּרֶךְ
b-**de**-rech	בְּדֶרֶךְ
ba	בָּהּ
ba-**hem**	בָּהֶם
b-**har**	בְּהַר
be-ha-**reem**	בֶּהָרִים
bo	בּוֹ
bo-a-**chem**	בּוֹאֲכֶם
bo-**ray**	בּוֹרֵא
b-**zot**	בְּזֹאת
ba-**ze**	בָּזֶה
baz-**man**	בַּזְּמַן
beez-**man**	בִּזְמַן
b-**chag**	בְּחַג
ba-**cho**-desh	בַּחֹדֶשׁ
b-**cho**-desh	בְּחֹדֶשׁ
b-cha-**yay**	בְּחַיֵּי
b-cha-yay-**chon**	בְּחַיֵּיכוֹן
ba-cha-**yeem**	בַּחַיִּים
b-chem-**la**	בְּחֶמְלָה
b-**chayn**	בְּחֵן
b-**che**-sed	בְּחֶסֶד
b-**chas**-dcha	בְּחַסְדְּךָ
b-chas-**de**-cha	בְּחַסְדֶּךָ
b-chef-**tso**	בְּחֶפְצוֹ
ba-**char**	בָּחַר

א ב ג ד ה ו ז ח ט י כ ל מ נ ס ע פ צ ק ר ש ת

בְּמֹשֶׁה	b-mo-**she**
בַּמִּשְׁפָּט	ba-meesh-**pat**
בְּמִשְׁפָּט	b-meesh-**pat**
בֵּן	**bayn**
בֶּן	**ben**
בָּנוּ	**ba**-noo
בְּנֵי	b-**nay**
בְּנֵיהֶם	b-nay-**hem**
בָּנָיו	ba-**nav**
בַּנֶיךָ	ba-**ne**-cha
בַּסֵּפֶר	ba-**say**-fer
בְּסֵפֶר	b-**say**-fer
בַּעֲגָלָא	ba-a-**ga**-la
בָּעוֹלָם	ba-o-**lam**
בְּעוֹז	b-**oz**
בְּעֶזְרַת	b-ez-**rat**
בְּעֵינֵי	b-ay-**nay**
בְּעֵינֶיךָ	b-ay-**ne**-cha
בְּעֵינֵינוּ	b-ay-**nay**-noo
בָּעִיר	ba-**eer**
בְּעִיר	b-**eer**
בַּעַל	**ba**-al
בְּעָלְמָא	b-ol-**ma**
בָּעָם	ba-**am**
בְּעַם	b-**am**
בְּעַמּוֹ	b-a-**mo**
בָּעַמִּים	ba-a-**meem**
בְּעַמְּךָ	b-am-**cha**
בְּעַמֶּךָ	b-a-**me**-cha
בֶּעָפָר	be-a-**far**
בָּעֶרֶב	ba-**e**-rev
בְּעֶרֶב	b-**e**-rev
בָּעֵת	ba-**ayt**
בְּעֵת	b-**ayt**
בְּפִי	b-**fee**
בִּפְנֵי	beef-**nay**
בְּצֶדֶק	b-**tse**-dek
בִּצְדָקָה	beets-da-**ka**
בְּצִיּוֹן	b-tsee-**yon**
בַּצָּרָה	ba-tsa-**ra**
בְּצָרָה	b-tsa-**ra**
בַּקֹּדֶשׁ	ba-**ko**-desh
בְּקָדְשׁוֹ	b-kod-**sho**
בְּקוֹל	b-**kol**
בְּקוּמֶךָ	b-koo-**me**-cha
בֹּקֶר	**bo**-ker
בְּקָרוֹב	b-ka-**rov**
בַּר מִצְוָה	**bar** meets-**va**
בָּרָא	ba-**ra**
בְּרָא	b-**ra**
בְּרֹאשׁ הַשָּׁנָה	b-**rosh** ha-sha-**na**
בְּרֵאשִׁית	b-ray-**sheet**
בְּרוּחַ	b-**roo**-ach
בָּרוּךְ	ba-**rooch**
בְּרַחֲמָיו	b-ra-cha-**mav**
בְּרַחֲמֶיךָ	b-ra-cha-**me**-cha
בְּרַחֲמִים	b-ra-cha-**meem**
בְּרִיךְ	b-**reech**
בְּרִית	**breet**
בֶּרֶךְ	**be**-rech
בְּרָכָה	b-ra-**cha**
בָּרְכוּ	bar-**choo**
בָּרְכוּנִי	bar-**choo**-nee
בָּרְכֵנוּ	bar-**chay**-noo
בִּרְכָתָא	beer-**cha**-ta
בְּרִנָּה	b-ree-**na**
בְּרָצוֹן	b-ra-**tson**
בִּרְצוֹנְךָ	beer-tson-**cha**
בִּרְצוֹנֶךָ	beer-tso-**ne**-cha
בַּשְּׁבִיעִי	ba-shvee-**ee**
בַּשַּׁבָּת	ba-sha-**bat**
בְּשִׁבְתְּךָ	b-**sheev**-t-cha
בְּשִׁיר	b-**sheer**
בְּשָׁכְבְּךָ	b-**shoch**-b-cha
בַּשָּׁלוֹם	ba-sha-**lom**
בְּשָׁלוֹם	b-sha-**lom**
בִּשְׁלוֹמֶךָ	beesh-lo-**me**-cha
בְּשֵׁם	b-**shaym**
בִּשְׁמוֹ	beesh-**mo**
בִּשְׁמֵי	beesh-**may**
בִּשְׁמַיָּא	beesh-**ma**-ya
בַּשָּׁמַיִם	ba-sha-**ma**-yeem
בְּשִׁמְךָ	b-sheem-**cha**
בִּשְׁמֶךָ	beesh-**me**-cha
בַּשָּׁנָה	ba-sha-**na**
בִּשְׁעָרֶיךָ	beesh-a-**re**-cha
בְּשִׂמְחָה	b-seem-**cha**
בָּשָׂר	ba-**sar**
בְּשַׂר	b-**sar**
בְּשָׂשׂוֹן	b-sa-**son**
בַּת	**bat**
בַּת מִצְוָה	**bat** meets-**va**
בְּתֵבֵל	b-tay-**vayl**
בִּתְהִלָּה	beet-hee-**la**
בִּתְהִלָּתֶךָ	beet-hee-la-**te**-cha
בְּתוֹכֵנוּ	b-to-**chay**-noo
בַּתּוֹרָה	ba-to-**ra**
בְּתוֹרַת	b-to-**rat**
בְּתוֹרָתוֹ	b-to-ra-**to**
בְּתוֹרָתְךָ	b-to-rat-**cha**
בְּתוֹרָתֶךָ	b-to-ra-**te**-cha
בְּתִפְאָרָה	b-teef-a-**ra**

ב·ג·ד·ה

א ב ג ד ה ו ז ח ט י כ ל מ נ ס ע פ צ ק ר ש ת

b-teef-**e**-ret . . . . . בְּתִפְאֶרֶת

ג

g-oo-**leem** . . . . גְּאוּלִים
ga-**al** . . . . גָּאַל
g-oo-**la** . . . . גְּאֻלָּה
go-a-**lee** . . . . גֹּאֲלִי
go-a-**lay**-noo . . . . . . גֹּאֲלֵנוּ
gee-**bor** . . . . . . גִּבֹּר, גִּבּוֹר
g-voo-**rot** . גְּבוּרוֹת, גְּבוּרֹת
ga-**dol** . . . . גָּדוֹל, גָּדֹל
g-doo-**la** . . . . גְּדֻלָּה
god-**le**-cha . . . . גָּדְלֶךָ
go-**ayl** . . . . גּוֹאֵל, גֹּאֵל
go-a-**lee** . . . . . גּוֹאֲלִי, גֹּאֲלִי
goi . . . . גּוֹי
goi-**yeem** . . . . גּוֹיִם
g-vee-ya-**tee** . . . . גְּוִיָּתִי
go-**mayl** . . . . גּוֹמֵל
gee-loo-**leem** . . . . . גִּלּוּלִים
gam . . . . גַּם
go-ra-**lay**-noo . . . . . . גּוֹרָלֵנוּ

ד

da-a-mee-**ran** . . . . . דַּאֲמִירָן
da-**var** . . . . דָּבָר
de-ver . . . . דֶּבֶר
d-**var** . . . . דְּבַר
deev-**ray** . . . . דִּבְרֵי
d-va-**reem** . . . . דְּבָרִים
dee-**bar**-ta . . . . דִּבַּרְתָּ
da-**veed** . . . . דָּוִד, דָּוִיד
do-**dee** . . . . דּוֹדִי
do-**me** . . . . דּוֹמֶה

dor . . . . דּוֹר, דֹּר
dee . . . . דַּי
d-**chal** . . . . דְּכָל
da . . . . דַּע
da-at . . . . דַּעַת, דָּעַת
d-**kood**-sha . דְּקֻדְשָׁא, דְּקוּדְשָׁא
dor . . . . דֹּר, דּוֹר
de-rech . . . . דֶּרֶךְ
dar-**chay** . . . . דַּרְכֵי
d-ra-**che**-ha . . . . דְּרָכֶיהָ

ה

ha . . . . הַ, הָ, הֲ
he . . . . הֶ
ha-**av** . . . . הָאָב
ha-a-**dam** . . . . הָאָדָם
ha-a-da-**ma** . . . . הָאֲדָמָה
ha-a-ha-**va** . . . . הָאַהֲבָה
ha-o-**mayr** . . . . הָאוֹמֵר
ha-e-**chad** . . . . הָאֶחָד
ha-**eesh** . . . . הָאִישׁ
ha-**ay**-le . . . . הָאֵלֶּה
ha-e-**met** . . . . הָאֱמֶת
ha-a-soo-**reem** . . . . הָאֲסוּרִים
ha-**a**-rets . . . . הָאָרֶץ
ha-a-ra-**tsot** . . . . הָאֲרָצוֹת
ha-**aysh** . . . . הָאֵשׁ
ha-**ba** . . . . הַבָּא
ha-voo . . . . הָבוּ
ha-bo-**ray** . . . . הַבּוֹרֵא
ha-**bayn** . . . . הַבֵּן
ha-**bo**-ker . . . . הַבֹּקֶר
ha-**breet** . . . . הַבְּרִית
ha-bra-**cha** . . . . הַבְּרָכָה

ha-go-**ayl** . . . . הַגֹּאֵל
ha-gee-**bor** . . . . הַגִּבּוֹר
ha-g-voo-**ra** . . . . . . הַגְּבוּרָה
ha-g-voo-**rot** . . . . . הַגְּבוּרוֹת
ha-ga-**da** . . . . הַגָּדָה
ha-ga-**dol** . . . . הַגָּדוֹל
ha-gdoo-**la** . . . . הַגְּדֻלָּה
ha-**goi** . . . . הַגּוֹי
ha-goi-**yeem** . . . . הַגּוֹיִם
ha-go-**mayl** . . . . הַגּוֹמֵל
heg-**yon** . . . . הֶגְיוֹן
hee-gee-**a**-noo . . . . . הִגִּיעָנוּ
ha-**ga**-fen . . . . הַגָּפֶן
ha-da-**var** . . . . הַדָּבָר
ha-d-va-**reem** . . . . . הַדְּבָרִים
ho-**dot** . . . . . הֹדוֹת, הוֹדוֹת
ha-**da**-at . . . . הַדַּעַת
ha-**de**-rech . . . . הַדֶּרֶךְ
ha-**hoo** . . . . ההוּא
ha-**hod** . . . . ההוֹד
ha-**hee** . . . . ההִיא
ha-**haym** . . . . הָהֵם
he-ha-**reem** . . . . הֶהָרִים
hoo . . . . הוּא
ho-da-**ot** . . . . הוֹדָאוֹת
ho-**doo** . . . . הוֹדוּ
ho-**dot** . . . . . הוֹדוֹת, הֹדוֹת
ho-**ve** . . . . הוֹוֶה
ho-shee-**ay**-noo . . . הוֹשִׁיעֵנוּ
ho-**sha** . . . . הוֹשַׁע
ha-**zot** . . . . הַזֹּאת
ha-**ze** . . . . הַזֶּה
ha-zo-**chayr** . . . . הַזּוֹכֵר
ha-zee-ka-**ron** . . . . . הַזִּכָּרוֹן

ה

א ב ג ד ה ו ז ח ט י כ ל מ נ ס ע פ צ ק ר ש ת

ha-**cho**-desh	הַחֹדֶשׁ
ha-cha-**yeem**	הַחַיִּים
ha-**che**-sed	הַחֶסֶד
ha-**cho**-shech	הַחֹשֶׁךְ
ha-**tov**	הַטּוֹב
ha-to-**va**	הַטּוֹבָה
ha-to-**veem**	הַטּוֹבִים
hee	הִיא
ha-**yad**	הַיָּד
ha-**ya**	הָיָה
ha-**yoo**	הָיוּ
ha-**yom**	הַיּוֹם
ha-yo-**tsayr**	הַיּוֹצֵר
ha-**yam**	הַיָּם
ha-ya-**meem**	הַיָּמִים
ha-y-shoo-**a**	הַיְשׁוּעָה
ha-ka-**vod**	הַכָּבוֹד
ha-**kol**	הַכֹּל
ha-ka-**la**	הַכַּלָּה
ha-ka-**toov**	הַכָּתוּב
ha-**layv**	הַלֵּב
ha-lay-**vav**	הַלֵּבָב
ha-**lai**-la	הַלַּיְלָה
ha-lay-**lot**	הַלֵּילוֹת
ha-l-loo-**hoo**	הַלְלוּהוּ
haym	הֵם
ham-va-**raych**	הַמְבָרֵךְ
ham-vo-**rach**	הַמְבֹרָךְ
ha-ma-**gayn**	הַמָּגֵן
ha-mo-**nam**	הֲמוֹנָם
ha-**mo**-tsee	הַמּוֹצִיא
ha-mo-**shee**-a	הַמּוֹשִׁיעַ
ham-ya-cha-**deem**	הַמְיַחֲדִים
ha-**ma**-yeem	הַמַּיִם

heem-**lee**-choo	הִמְלִיכוּ
ha-**me**-lech	הַמֶּלֶךְ
ha-mal-**choot**	הַמַּלְכוּת
ham-la-**cheem**	הַמְּלָכִים
ha-**mam**-la-cha	הַמַּמְלָכָה
ham-noo-**cha**	הַמְּנוּחָה
ha-ma-a-**se**	הַמַּעֲשֶׂה
ha-mats-**mee**-ach	הַמַּצְמִיחַ
ha-mak-dee-**sheem**	הַמַּקְדִּישִׁים
ha-ma-**kom**	הַמָּקוֹם
ham-ka-**yaym**	הַמְקַיֵּם
ham-ra-**chaym**	הַמְרַחֵם
ha-meesh-**pat**	הַמִּשְׁפָּט
ha-mees-**ra**	הַמִּשְׂרָה
ha-may-**teem**	הַמֵּתִים
ha-ma-**teer**	הַמַּתִּיר
ha-meet-na-**say**	הַמִּתְנַשֵּׂא
ha-ne-e-**man**	הַנֶּאֱמָן
hee-**nay**	הִנֵּה
ha-nof-**leem**	הַנּוֹפְלִים
ha-no-**ra**	הַנּוֹרָא
ha-no-**tayn**	הַנּוֹתֵן
heen-chee-**la**-noo	הִנְחִילָנוּ
heen-chal-**ta**-noo	הִנְחַלְתָּנוּ
ha-**nay**-tsach	הַנֵּצַח
ha-so-**maych**	הַסּוֹמֵךְ
ha-o-**lam**	הָעוֹלָם
ha-o-la-**meem**	הָעוֹלָמִים
ha-o-**say**	הָעוֹשֶׂה
ha-**oz**	הָעֹז
ha-el-**yon**	הָעֶלְיוֹן
ha-**am**	הָעָם
ha-a-**meem**	הָעַמִּים
ha-**o**-mer	הָעֹמֶר

he-a-**far**	הֶעָפָר
ha-o-**se**	הָעֹשֶׂה
ha-tsa-**deek**	הַצַּדִּיק
ha-tsa-dee-**keem**	הַצַּדִּיקִים
ha-**tse**-dek	הַצֶּדֶק
ha-ts-da-**ka**	הַצְּדָקָה
ha-**tsoor**	הַצּוּר
ha-tsa-**ra**	הַצָּרָה
ha-ka-**dosh**	הַקָּדוֹשׁ
ha-kdo-**sheem**	הַקְּדוֹשִׁים
ha-**ko**-desh	הַקֹּדֶשׁ
har	הַר
ha-**rav**	הָרָב
ha-ra-**beem**	הָרַבִּים
ha-**roo**-ach	הָרוּחַ
ha-ro-**fay**	הָרוֹפֵא
ha-ra-cha-**meem**	הָרַחֲמִים
ha-ra-cha-**man**	הָרַחֲמָן
ha-**reem**	הָרִים
ha-**raym**	הָרֵם
ha-**ra**	הָרָע
ha-ra-**a**	הָרָעָה
ha-r-sha-**eem**	הָרְשָׁעִים
hash-vee-**ee**	הַשְּׁבִיעִי
ha-sha-**bat**	הַשַּׁבָּת
ha-shay-vo-**ta**	הֲשֵׁבֹתָ
ha-sho-**mayr**	הַשּׁוֹמֵר
ha-shee-**vay**-noo	הֲשִׁיבֵנוּ
ha-**sheer**	הַשִּׁיר
ha-sha-**lom**	הַשָּׁלוֹם
ha-**shaym**	הַשֵּׁם
ha-sha-**ma**-yeem	הַשָּׁמַיִם
ha-sha-**na**	הַשָּׁנָה
ha-shee-**shee**	הַשִּׁשִּׁי

ה·ו·ז·ח·ט·י

א ב ג ד ה ו ז ח ט י כ ל מ נ ס ע פ צ ק ר ש ת

הַתּוֹרָה . . . ha-to-**ra**
הַתִּפְאֶרֶת . . . ha-teef-e-ret

ו

וְ . . . **v**
וּ . . . **oo**
וָ, וַ . . . **va**
וֶ . . . **ve**
וֵ . . . **vay**
וְאָהַבְתָּ . . . v-a-**hav**-ta
וְדִבַּרְתָּ . . . v-dee-**bar**-ta
וְהָיָה . . . v-ha-**ya**
וְהָיוּ . . . v-ha-**yoo**
וַהֲשֵׁבֹתָ . . . va-ha-shay-vo-**ta**
וַיְבָרֵךְ . . . va-y-**va**-raych
וְיָדַעְתָּ . . . v-ya-**da**-ta
וַיְהִי . . . va-y-**hee**
וִיהִיוּ . . . v-yee-**hyoo**
וַיְכַל . . . va-y-**chal**
וַיְכֻלּוּ . . . va-y-**choo**-loo
וַיִּמְלֹךְ . . . va-**yeem**-loch
וַיִּנָּפַשׁ . . . va-yee-na-**fash**
וַיְקַדֵּשׁ . . . va-y-**ka**-daysh
וַיִּשְׁבֹּת . . . va-yeesh-**bot**
וּכְתַבְתָּם . . . ooch-**tav**-tam
וָעֶד . . . va-**ed**
וְצִוָּנוּ . . . v-tsee-**va**-noo
וּקְשַׁרְתָּם . . . ook-**shar**-tam
וְשָׁמְרוּ . . . v-**sham**-roo
וְשִׁנַּנְתָּם . . . v-shee-**nan**-tam

ז

זֹאת . . . **zot**
זֶה . . . **ze**
זוֹכֵר . . . zo-**chayr**
זוּלָתוֹ . . . zoo-la-**to**
זֵכֶר . . . **zay**-cher
זִכָּרוֹן . . . zee-ka-**ron**
זִכְרוֹן . . . zee-**chron**
זָכְרֵנוּ . . . zoch-**ray**-noo
זְמַן . . . **zman**

ח

חֶבְלִי . . . chev-**lee**
חַג, חָג . . . **chag**
חָדֵשׁ . . . cha-**daysh**
חֹדֶשׁ . . . **cho**-desh
חֲדָשָׁה . . . cha-da-**sha**
חוֹלִים . . . cho-**leem**
חַזָּן . . . cha-**zan**
חָזָק . . . cha-**zak**
חֵטְא . . . **chayt**
חָטָאנוּ . . . cha-**ta**-noo
חַי . . . **chai**
חַיֵּי . . . cha-**yay**
חַיִּים . . . cha-**yeem**
חַיֵּינוּ . . . cha-**yay**-noo
חַלָּה . . . cha-**la**
חֶלְקֵנוּ . . . chel-**kay**-noo
חָמוֹל . . . cha-**mol**
חָמֵץ . . . cha-**mayts**
חֵן . . . **chayn**
חַנּוּן . . . cha-**noon**
חֲנֻכָּה . . . cha-noo-**ka**
חֲנֻכִּיָּה . . . cha-noo-kee-**ya**
חָנֵּנוּ . . . cha-**nay**-noo
חֶסֶד . . . **che**-sed
חַסְדּוֹ . . . chas-**do**
חַסְדֵי . . . chas-**day**
חֲסָדִים . . . cha-sa-**deem**
חַסְדְּךָ . . . chas-d-**cha**
חַסְדֶּךָ . . . chas-**de**-cha
חֶרֶב . . . **che**-rev
חָרָה אַף . . . cha-**ra af**
חֹשֶׁךְ . . . **cho**-shech

ט

ט״וּ בִּשְׁבָט . . . **too** bee-**shvat**
טוֹב . . . **tov**
טוֹבָה, טֹבָה . . . to-**va**
טוֹבִים . . . to-**veem**
טוּבְךָ . . . **toov**-cha
טוּבֶךָ . . . too-**ve**-cha
טַלִּית . . . ta-**leet**
טַפֵּנוּ . . . ta-**pay**-noo

י

יֹאמְרוּ . . . yo-**may**-roo
יָבוֹא, יָבֹא . . . ya-**vo**
יְבָרֵךְ . . . y-va-**raych**
יְבָרֶךְ . . . y-va-**rech**
יַגִּיד . . . ya-**geed**
יָד . . . **yad**
יַד . . . **yad**
יְדֵי . . . y-**day**
יָדְךָ . . . yad-**cha**
יָדֶךָ . . . ya-**de**-cha
יֵדְעוּ . . . yayd-**oo**
יָדַעְתָּ . . . ya-**da**-ta
יְהֵא . . . y-**hay**
יְהוּדָה . . . y-hoo-**da**
יְהִי . . . y-**hee**

י · כ

- yee-h-**ye** . . . יִהְיֶה
- yee-h-**yoo** . . . יִהְיוּ
- y-ha-l-**loo**-cha . . . יְהַלְלוּךָ
- yo-**doo**-cha . . . יוֹדוּךָ, יוֹדֶךָ
- **yom** . . . יוֹם
- **yom** kee-**poor** . . . יוֹם כִּפּוּר
- yo-**sayd** . . . יוֹסֵד
- yo-**tsayr** . . . יוֹצֵר
- yosh-**vay** . . . יוֹשְׁבֵי, יֹשְׁבֵי
- yosh-**veen** . . . יוֹשְׁבִין
- **ya**-chad . . . יַחַד
- ya-**chon** . . . יָחֹן
- ya-**kee**-roo . . . יַכִּירוּ
- y-**chal** . . . יְכַל
- y-**choo**-loo . . . יְכֻלוּ
- yeech-r-**oo** . . . יִכְרְעוּ
- **yam** . . . יָם
- ya-**moosh** . . . יָמוּשׁ
- y-**may** . . . יְמֵי
- ya-**meem** . . . יָמִים
- ya-**may**-noo . . . יָמֵינוּ
- y-**meen**-cha . . . יְמִינְךָ
- y-mee-**ne**-cha . . . יְמִינֶךָ
- yeem-**loch** . . . יִמְלוֹךְ, יִמְלֹךְ
- yam-**leech** . . . יַמְלִיךְ
- yee-na-**fash** . . . יִנָּפַשׁ
- ya-a-**mod** . . . יַעֲמֹד
- ya-a-**kov** . . . יַעֲקֹב, יַעֲקוֹב
- ya-a-**se** . . . יַעֲשֶׂה
- yee-**po**-loo . . . יִפֹּלוּ
- **yee**-fen . . . יִפֶן
- yeets-**chak** . . . יִצְחָק
- y-**tseer** . . . יְצִיר
- y-kab-**loo** . . . יְקַבְּלוּ
- y-ka-**daysh** . . . יְקַדֵּשׁ
- y-**kar** . . . יְקָר
- yeek-r-**oo** . . . יִקְרְאוּ
- y-ka-**ro** . . . יְקָרוֹ
- yeer-**a** . . . יִרְאָה
- y-roo-sha-**la**-yeem . . . יְרוּשָׁלַיִם, יְרוּשָׁלָיִם, יְרוּשָׁלָם
- y-ra-**kot** . . . יְרָקוֹת
- yosh-**vay** . . . יֹשְׁבֵי, יוֹשְׁבֵי
- yeesh-**bot** . . . יִשְׁבֹּת
- y-shoo-**a** . . . יְשׁוּעָה
- y-shoo-at-**cha** . . . יְשׁוּעָתְךָ
- y-shoo-a-**te**-cha . . . יְשׁוּעָתֶךָ
- yash-mee-**ay**-noo . . . יַשְׁמִיעֵנוּ
- yeesh-ay-**noo** . . . יִשְׁעֵנוּ
- yeesh-ta-**bach** . . . יִשְׁתַּבַּח
- yees-ra-**ayl** . . . יִשְׂרָאֵל
- yeet-ba-**rach** . . . יִתְבָּרַךְ
- yeet-ga-**dal** . . . יִתְגַּדַּל
- yeet-ha-**dar** . . . יִתְהַדַּר
- yeet-ha-**lal** . . . יִתְהַלַּל
- yee-**tayn** . . . יִתֵּן
- yee-**tay**-noo . . . יִתֵּנוּ
- yeet-na-**say** . . . יִתְנַשֵּׂא
- yeet-a-**le** . . . יִתְעַלֶּה
- yeet-pa-**ar** . . . יִתְפָּאַר
- yeet-ka-**dash** . . . יִתְקַדַּשׁ
- yeet-ro-**mam** . . . יִתְרוֹמַם

כ

- **k** . . . כְּ
- **ka** . . . כַּ, כָּ
- **ke** . . . כֶּ
- **kee** . . . כִּ
- **kay** . . . כֵּ
- k-**av** . . . כְּאָב
- k-a-**dam** . . . כְּאָדָם
- k-**or** . . . כְּאוֹר
- k-e-**chad** . . . כְּאֶחָד
- k-**eesh** . . . כְּאִישׁ
- ka-**ay**-le . . . כָּאֵלֶּה
- k-**aysh** . . . כְּאֵשׁ
- ka-**vod** . . . כָּבוֹד
- k-**vod** . . . כְּבוֹד
- k-vo-**do** . . . כְּבוֹדוֹ
- k-vo-**de**-cha . . . כְּבוֹדֶךָ
- keev-**nay** . . . כִּבְנֵי
- k-gee-**bor** . . . כְּגִבּוֹר
- k-goi-**yay** . . . כְּגוֹיֵי
- ka-da-**var** . . . כַּדָּבָר
- keed-**var** . . . כִּדְבַר
- ka-**hem** . . . כָּהֶם
- ko-**hayn** . . . כֹּהֵן
- k-**har** . . . כְּהַר
- koo-**lam** . . . כּוּלָּם, כֻּלָּם
- ko-**see** . . . כּוֹסִי
- kor-**eem** . . . כּוֹרְעִים
- k-chas-d-**cha** . . . כְּחַסְדְּךָ
- k-chas-**de**-cha . . . כְּחַסְדֶּךָ
- **kee** . . . כִּי
- ka-**yom** . . . כַּיּוֹם
- k-**yom** . . . כְּיוֹם
- ka-**yam** . . . כַּיָּם
- kee-**may** . . . כִּימֵי
- kee-roo-sha-**la**-yeem . . . כִּירוּשָׁלַיִם
- k-**chol** . . . כְּכָל
- k-**chol** . . . כְּכֹל
- ka-ka-**la** . . . כַּכַּלָּה

keech-**lot** . . . . כִּכְלוֹת
ka-ka-**toov** . . . . כַּכָּתוּב
kol . . . . כָּל
kol . . . . כֹּל
ka-**la** . . . . כַּלָּה
ka-**lay** . . . . כַּלֵּה
koo-**lo** . . . . כֻּלּוֹ
koo-**lam** . . . . . . כֻּלָּם, כּוּלָּם
koo-**la**-noo . . . . כֻּלָּנוּ
k-**mo** . . . . כְּמוֹ
ka-**mo**-cha . . . כָּמוֹךָ, כָּמוֹכָה
k-mo-shee-**ay**-noo . כְּמוֹשִׁיעֵנוּ
k-mal-**kay**-noo . . . . . כְּמַלְכֵּנוּ
k-ma-a-**se**-cha . . . . כְּמַעֲשֶׂיךָ
k-mo-**she** . . . . כְּמֹשֶׁה
k-meesh-p-**chot** . . כְּמִשְׁפְּחוֹת
kayn . . . . כֵּן
kee-noom-**cha** . . . . . כִּנְאֻמְךָ
k-**sod see**-ach . . . כְּסוֹד שִׂיחַ
k-am-**cha** . . . . כְּעַמְּךָ
k-a-**me**-cha . . . . כְּעַמֶּךָ
ke-a-**far** . . . . כֶּעָפָר
kee-**pa** . . . . כִּפָּה
k-**fee** . . . . כְּפִי
ka-**per** . . . . כַּפֵּר
k-**ke**-dem . . . . כְּקֶדֶם
. . . . כָּרוֹת יִכָּרֵתוּן
ka-**rot** yee-ka-ray-**toon**
k-ra-**chaym** . . . . כְּרַחֵם
keer-oo-**tay** . . . . . . כִּרְעוּתֵהּ
k-she-a-**dam** . . . . . . כְּשֶׁאָדָם
k-she-a-**nee** . . . . . . כְּשֶׁאֲנִי
k-she-a-**ta** . . . . כְּשֶׁאַתָּה
k-she-**hoo** . . . . כְּשֶׁהוּא

k-she-ha-**ya** . . . . . . כְּשֶׁהָיָה
k-she-yee-h-**yoo** . . . . כְּשֶׁיִּהְיוּ
k-she-**lach** . . . . כְּשֶׁלָּךְ
k-**shaym** . . . . כְּשֵׁם
kee-**shmo** . . . . כִּשְׁמוֹ
k-sheem-**cha** . . . . . . כְּשִׁמְךָ
keesh-**me**-cha . . . . . . כְּשִׁמֶךָ
ka-**sher** . . . . כָּשֵׁר
kat-**vay**-noo . . . . כָּתְבֵנוּ
k-tav-**tam** . . . . כְּתַבְתָּם
ka-**toov** . . . . כָּתוּב
k-too-**ba** . . . . כְּתוּבָּה
ka-to-**ra** . . . . כַּתּוֹרָה

ל

l . . . . לְ
la . . . . לַ, לָ
le . . . . לֶ
lee . . . . לִ
lay . . . . לֵ
lo . . . . לֹא
la-a-vo-**tay**-noo . . . לַאֲבוֹתֵינוּ
l-av-ra-**ham** . . . . . לְאַבְרָהָם
la-a-**don** . . . . לַאֲדוֹן
l-a-**dam** . . . . לְאָדָם
lay-**a** . . . . לֵאָה
l-**ot** . . . . לְאוֹת
l-**ayn** . . . . לְאֵין
l-**eesh** . . . . לְאִישׁ
la-**ay**-le . . . . לָאֵלֶּה
lay-**mor** . . . . לֵאמֹר
la-a-rets . . . . לָאָרֶץ
la-a-**sher** . . . . לַאֲשֶׁר
layv . . . . לֵב

l-**vav** . . . . לְבַב
lay-**vav** . . . . לֵבָב
l-vav-**cha** . . . . לְבָבְךָ
l-va-**ve**-cha . . . . לְבָבֶךָ
l-va-**do** . . . . לְבַדּוֹ
lee-**bee** . . . . לִבִּי
l-**vayt** . . . . לְבֵית
l-vayt-**cha** . . . . לְבֵיתְךָ
l-vay-**te**-cha . . . . . . לְבֵיתֶךָ
lee-**bam** . . . . לִבָּם
l-**ven** . . . . לְבֵן
lee-**bay**-noo . . . . לִבֵּנוּ
leev-**nay** . . . . לִבְנֵי
leev-nay-**hem** . . . . . לִבְנֵיהֶם
l-va-**ne**-cha . . . . לְבָנֶיךָ
la-**bo**-ker . . . . לַבֹּקֶר
la-**breet** . . . . לַבְּרִית
leev-**reet** . . . . לִבְרִית
l-va-**raych** . . . . לְבָרֵךְ
leev-ra-**cha** . . . . . . לִבְרָכָה
l-va-**sar** . . . . לְבָשָׂר
la-goi-**yeem** . . . . לַגּוֹיִם
l-da-**veed** . . . . לְדָוִד
l-do-**dee** . . . . לְדוֹדִי
l-**dor** va-**dor** . . . . לְדוֹר וָדוֹר
la-**da**-at . . . . לָדַעַת
l-do-ro-**tam** . . . . . . לְדֹרֹתָם
l-had-**leek** . . . . לְהַדְלִיק
l-ho-**dot** . . . . לְהוֹדוֹת
l-ho-**shee**-a . . . . . . לְהוֹשִׁיעַ
l-hach-bee-**ra** . . . . לְהַחְבִּירָה
l-ha-cha-**yot** . . . . . . לְהַחֲיוֹת
lee-h-**yot** . . . . לִהְיוֹת
la-**hem** . . . . לָהֶם

א ב ג ד ה ו ז ח ט י כ ל מ נ ס ע פ צ ק ר ש ת

l-av-d-**cha**	לְעַבְדְּךָ
l-av-**de**-cha	לְעַבְדֶּךָ
la-**ad**	לָעַד
l-o-**lam**	לְעוֹלָם, לְעֹלָם
la-o-**lam**	לָעוֹלָם
l-o-**lam** va-**ed**	לְעוֹלָם וָעֶד
l-ol-**may ad**	לְעוֹלְמֵי עַד
l-o-la-**meem**	לְעוֹלָמִים
l-o-**say**	לְעוֹשֵׂה
l-ay-**nay**	לְעֵינֵי
l-ay-**nay**-noo	לְעֵינֵינוּ
l-**ay**-la	לְעֵלָּא
l-o-**lam**	לְעֹלָם
l-ol-**may**	לְעָלְמֵי
la-**am**	לָעָם
l-**am**	לְעָם, לְעַם
l-a-**mo**	לְעַמּוֹ
l-am-**cha**	לְעַמְּךָ
l-a-**me**-cha	לְעַמֶּךָ
la-**o**-mer	לָעֹמֶר
l-oo-**mat**	לְעֻמַּת
l-oo-ma-**tam**	לְעֻמָּתָם
le-a-**far**	לֶעָפָר
l-a-**far**	לְעָפָר
l-o-**se**	לְעֹשֶׂה
la-a-**sot**	לַעֲשׂוֹת
l-**ayt**	לְעֵת
l-**fee**	לְפִי
leef-**nay**	לִפְנֵי
l-fa-**nav**	לְפָנָיו
l-fa-**ne**-cha	לְפָנֶיךָ
la-tsa-**deek**	לַצַּדִּיק
la-tsa-dee-**keem**	לַצַּדִּיקִים
leets-da-**ka**	לִצְדָקָה

lee-shay-**nay**	לִישֵׁנֵי
l-yees-ra-**ayl**	לְיִשְׂרָאֵל
lach	לָךְ
l-**cha**	לְךָ
leech-**vod**	לִכְבוֹד
l-cha-**vod**	לְכָבוֹד
l-**cha**	לְכָה
l-**cha** do-**dee**	לְכָה דוֹדִי
la-**kol**	לַכֹּל
l-**chol**	לְכָל
l-**chol**	לְכֹל
l-choo-**lam**	לְכֻלָּם
la-**chem**	לָכֶם
l-mo-shee-**ay**-noo	לְמוֹשִׁיעֵנוּ
la-ma-cha-zee-**keem**	לַמַּחֲזִיקִים
la-**me**-lech	לַמֶּלֶךְ
l-**me**-lech	לְמֶלֶךְ
l-mal-choot-**cha**	לְמַלְכוּתְךָ
l-mal-choo-**te**-cha	לְמַלְכוּתֶךָ
lam-la-**cheem**	לַמְּלָכִים
l-mal-**kay**-noo	לְמַלְכֵּנוּ
leem-noo-**cha**	לִמְנוּחָה
l-**ma**-an	לְמַעַן
l-ma-a-**say**	לְמַעֲשֵׂה
l-meets-vo-**tav**	לְמִצְוֹתָיו
l-meets-vo-**te**-cha	לְמִצְוֹתֶיךָ
la-ma-**kom**	לַמָּקוֹם
l-meek-ra-**ay ko**-desh	לְמִקְרָאֵי קֹדֶשׁ
la-ma-**rom**	לַמָּרוֹם
l-mo-**she**	לְמֹשֶׁה
l-meesh-**pat**	לְמִשְׁפָּט
la-noo	לָנוּ
l-naf-**shee**	לְנַפְשִׁי

l-ham-**sheel**	לְהַמְשִׁיל
l-ha-a-**veer**	לְהַעֲבִיר
l-haf-**not**	לְהַפְנוֹת
l-**har**	לְהַר
lo	לוֹ
lay-**vee**	לֵוִי
loo-**lav**	לוּלָב
l-**zay**-cher	לְזֵכֶר
l-zee-ka-**ron**	לְזִכָּרוֹן
laz-**man** ha-**ze**	לַזְּמַן הַזֶּה
la-**cho**-desh	לַחֹדֶשׁ
l-chai-**yeem**	לְחַיִּים
le-chem	לֶחֶם
l-**cho**-shech	לְחֹשֶׁךְ
la-**tov**	לַטּוֹב
l-**tov**	לְטוֹב
l-tov-**a**	לְטוֹבָה
la-to-**veem**	לַטּוֹבִים
l-to-ta-**fot**	לְטֹטָפֹת
lee	לִי
l-**yad**	לְיַד
lee-hoo-**da**	לִיהוּדָה
la-**yom**	לַיּוֹם
l-**yom**	לְיוֹם
l-yo-**tsayr**	לְיוֹצֵר
lai-la	לַיְלָה, לָיְלָה
l-ya-a-**kov**	לְיַעֲקֹב
l-yeets-**chak**	לְיִצְחָק
lee-tsee-**at**	לִיצִיאַת
l-yeer-**a**	לְיִרְאָה
lee-roo-sha-**la**-yeem	לִירוּשָׁלַיִם
lee-**shoo**-a	לִישׁוּעָה
lee-shoo-at-**cha**	לִישׁוּעָתְךָ
lee-shoo-a-**te**-cha	לִישׁוּעָתֶךָ

l-**tsoor**	לְצוּר
l-tsee-**yon**	לְצִיּוֹן
l-**ko**-desh	לְקֹדֶשׁ
l-kod-**sho**	לְקָדְשׁוֹ
l-**kol**	לְקוֹל
leek-**rat**	לִקְרַאת
la-ka-**rov**	לַקָּרוֹב
leer-**ot**	לִרְאוֹת
l-**rosh**	לְרֹאשׁ
l-ra-**chaym**	לְרַחֵם
l-ra-cha-**meem**	לְרַחֲמִים
la-**ra**	לָרָע
l-ra-**a**	לְרָעָה
l-ra-**tson**	לְרָצוֹן
la-r-sha-**eem**	לָרְשָׁעִים
l-sha-**bay**-ach	לְשַׁבֵּחַ
la-sha-**bat**	לַשַּׁבָּת
la-**shon**	לָשׁוֹן
l-sha-**lom**	לְשָׁלוֹם
l-sha-**laym**	לְשַׁלֵּם
l-**shaym**	לְשֵׁם
leesh-**mo**	לִשְׁמוֹ
la-sha-**ma**-yeem	לַשָּׁמַיִם
l-sheem-**cha**	לְשִׁמְךָ
leesh-**me**-cha	לִשְׁמֶךָ
leesh-**mor**	לִשְׁמֹר
l-sha-**na**	לְשָׁנָה
l-seem-**cha**	לְשִׂמְחָה
l-sa-**son**	לְשָׂשׂוֹן
leet-hee-**la**	לִתְהִלָּה
la-to-**ra**	לַתּוֹרָה
l-to-rat-**cha**	לְתוֹרָתְךָ
l-to-ra-**te**-cha	לְתוֹרָתֶךָ
l-ta-**meed**	לְתָמִיד
l-teef-**e**-ret	לְתִפְאֶרֶת
l-ta-**kayn**	לְתַקֵּן
la-**tayt**	לָתֵת

מ

mee	מִ
may	מֵ
m-**od**	מְאֹד
m-o-**de**-cha	מְאֹדֶךָ
may-a-**dam**	מֵאָדָם
may-**az**	מֵאָז
may-**ayn**	מֵאַיִן
may-**eesh**	מֵאִישׁ
may-**e**-rets	מֵאֶרֶץ
may-**aysh**	מֵאֵשׁ
may-a-**sher**	מֵאַשֶׁר
m-oo-**shar**	מְאֻשָּׁר
may-**vee**	מֵבִיא
mee-**bayn**	מִבֵּין
mee-**bayt**	מִבֵּית
mee-b-**nay**	מִבְּנֵי
m-va-**rach**	מְבָרַךְ
m-**vo**-rach	מְבֹרָךְ
mee-**goi**	מִגּוֹי
ma-**gayn**	מָגֵן
mee-deev-**ray**	מִדִּבְרֵי
ma	מַה, מָה
may-**har**	מֵהַר
m-hay-**ra**	מְהֵרָה
mo-**de**	מוֹדֶה
mo-**deem**	מוֹדִים
mo-**shav**	מוֹשַׁב
mo-**shee**-a	מוֹשִׁיעַ
mo-shee-**ay**-noo	מוֹשִׁיעֵנוּ
mee-**ze**	מִזֶּה
m-zoo-**za**	מְזוּזָה
m-zoo-**zot**	מְזֻזוֹת
ma-**zal tov**	מַזָּל טוֹב
meez-**mor** l-da-**veed**	מִזְמוֹר לְדָוִד
m-cha-**yay**	מְחַיֵּה
m-cha-**ye**	מְחַיֶּה
m-**chal**	מְחַל
may-**cho**-shech	מֵחֹשֶׁךְ
mat-bee-**leen**	מַטְבִּילִין
mee-toov-**cha**	מִטּוּבְךָ
mee-too-**ve**-cha	מִטּוּבֶךָ
mee	מִי
mee-**yad**	מִיָּד
mee-**yad**	מִיַּד
mee-**yom**	מִיּוֹם
ma-yeem	מַיִם, מָיִם
mee-**may**	מִימֵי
mee-ya-**meem**	מִיָּמִים
mee-meen-**cha**	מִימִינְךָ
mee-mee-**ne**-cha	מִימִינֶךָ
mee-ya-a-**kov**	מִיַּעֲקֹב
mee-roo-sha-**la**-yeem	מִירוּשָׁלַיִם
mee-**kol**	מִכָּל
mee-**kol**	מִכֹּל
m-chal-**kayl**	מְכַלְכֵּל
mee-koo-**lam**	מִכֻּלָּם
ma-**lay**	מָלֵא
m-**lo**	מְלֹא
mal-a-**chay**	מַלְאֲכֵי
m-lach-**to**	מְלַאכְתּוֹ
ma-**lach**	מָלַךְ
me-lech	מֶלֶךְ
mal-**choot**	מַלְכוּת

מ · נ

א ב ג ד ה ו ז ח ט י כ ל מ נ ס ע פ צ ק ר ש ת

Pronunciation	Hebrew
mal-choo-**tay**	מַלְכוּתֵהּ
mal-choo-**to**	מַלְכוּתוֹ
mal-choot-**cha**	מַלְכוּתְךָ
mal-choo-**te**-cha	מַלְכוּתֶךָ
mal-**chay**	מַלְכֵי
m-la-**cheem**	מְלָכִים
mal-**kay**-noo	מַלְכֵּנוּ
mee-leef-**nay**	מִלִּפְנֵי
meel-fa-**ne**-cha	מִלְּפָנֶיךָ
may-**meet**	מֵמִית
mee-**me**-lech	מִמֶּלֶךְ
mee-**me**-noo	מִמֶּנּוּ
mee-ma-**al**	מִמַּעַל
mee-meets-vo-**te**-cha	מִמִּצְוֹתֶיךָ
mee-meets-**ra**-yeem	מִמִּצְרַיִם
meem-ko-**mo**	מִמְּקוֹמוֹ
mee-ma-**rom**	מִמָּרוֹם
mem-**shal**-t-cha	מֶמְשַׁלְתְּךָ
meen	מִן
m-noo-**cha**	מְנוּחָה
ma-**nos**	מָנוֹס
m-no-**ra**	מְנוֹרָה
meen-**yan**	מִנְיָן
m-**nat** ko-**see**	מְנָת כּוֹסִי
m-soo-**been**	מְסֻבִּין
may-o-**lam**	מֵעוֹלָם
may-**al**	מֵעַל
may-a-**lai**	מֵעָלַי
may-a-**lay**-noo	מֵעָלֵינוּ
may-**am**	מֵעַם, מֵעָם
may-**eem**	מֵעִם
may-am-**cha**	מֵעַמְּךָ
may-a-**me**-cha	מֵעַמֶּךָ
may-a-**far**	מֵעָפָר
may-**e**-rev	מֵעֶרֶב
ma-a-**say**	מַעֲשֵׂה
ma-a-**se**	מַעֲשֶׂה
ma-a-**se**-cha	מַעֲשֶׂיךָ
ma-a-**seem**	מַעֲשִׂים
may-a-**ta**	מֵעַתָּה
mee-**pee**	מִפִּי
mee-**pee**-noo	מִפִּינוּ
meep-**nay**	מִפְּנֵי
mee-pa-**nav**	מִפָּנָיו
mee-pa-**ne**-cha	מִפָּנֶיךָ
ma-**tsa**	מַצָּה
m-tsav-**cha**	מְצַוְּךָ
mee-**tsoor**	מִצּוּר
meets-vo-**tav**	מִצְוֹתָיו
meets-vo-**te**-cha	מִצְוֹתֶיךָ
mee-tsee-**yon**	מִצִּיּוֹן
mats-**mee**-ach	מַצְמִיחַ
meets-**ra**-yeem	מִצְרַיִם, מִצְרָיִם
m-ka-**daysh**	מְקַדֵּשׁ
m-kad-**shay**	מְקַדְּשֵׁי, מְקָדְּשֵׁי
ma-**kom**	מָקוֹם
m-**kom**	מְקוֹם
m-ka-**yaym**	מְקַיֵּם
meek-**ra** **ko**-desh	מִקְרָא קֹדֶשׁ
meek-ra-**ay** **ko**-desh	מִקְרָאֵי קֹדֶשׁ
may-**rosh**	מֵרֹאשׁ
ma-**rom**	מָרוֹם
m-ro-**meem**	מְרוֹמִים
ma-**ror**	מָרוֹר
may-**ra**	מֵרָע
may-r-sha-**eem**	מֵרְשָׁעִים
mo-**she**	מֹשֶׁה
mee-**sheer**	מִשִּׁיר
meesh-**mo**	מִשְּׁמוֹ
mash-mee-**eem**	מַשְׁמִיעִים
meesh-**pat**	מִשְׁפָּט
meesh-**pat**	מִשְׁפַּט
m-shar-**tav**	מְשָׁרְתָיו
meesh-ta-cha-**veem**	מִשְׁתַּחֲוִים
mas-**teen**	מַשְׂטִין
mee-to-rat-**cha**	מִתּוֹרָתְךָ
mee-to-ra-**te**-cha	מִתּוֹרָתֶךָ
mee-**ta**-chat	מִתָּחַת
may-**teem**	מֵתִים
ma-**teer**	מַתִּיר
meet-nas-**eem**	מִתְנַשְּׂאִים

נ

Pronunciation	Hebrew
na	נָא
ne-**dar**	נֶאְדָּר
ne-e-**man**	נֶאֱמָן
ne-e-**mar**	נֶאֱמַר
n-vee-**e**-cha	נְבִיאֶךָ
neev-**ra**	נִבְרָא
na-**geed**	נַגִּיד
no-**de**	נוֹדֶה
no-**te**	נוֹטֶה
nof-**leem**	נוֹפְלִים, נֹפְלִים
no-**ra**	נוֹרָא
no-**tayn**	נוֹתֵן, נֹתֵן
ne-che-**ma**-ta	נֶחֱמָתָא
na-**ta**	נָטַע
nee-**see**	נִסִּי
nee-**seem**	נִסִּים
no-**am**	נֹעַם
na-a-**reets**-cha	נַעֲרִיצְךָ

נ·ס·ע·פ·צ

א ב ג ד ה ו ז ח ט י כ ל מ נ ס ע פ צ ק ר ש ת

na-a-**sa** . . . . נַעֲשָׂה

neef-lo-**te**-cha . . . . . נִפְלְאוֹתֶיךָ, נִפְלְאֹתֶיךָ

nof-**leem** . . נֹפְלִים, נוֹפְלִים

naf-**shee** . . . . נַפְשִׁי

naf-sh-**cha** . . . . נַפְשְׁךָ

n-tsa-**cheem** . . . . . . נְצָחִים

n-kab-**la** . . . . נְקַבְּלָה

nak-**deesh** . . . . נַקְדִּישׁ

nak-deesh-**cha** . . . . נַקְדִּישְׁךָ

n-ka-**daysh** . . . . נְקַדֵּשׁ

n-ka-**ve** . . . . נְקַוֶּה

neek-**ra** . . . . נִקְרָא

nayr . . . . נֵר

na-**shoo**-va . . . . . . נָשׁוּבָה

neesh-ma-**tee** . . . . . נִשְׁמָתִי

neesh-ta-**na** . . . . . . נִשְׁתַּנָּה

n-tee-vo-**te**-ha . . . . נְתִבוֹתֶיהָ

na-**tan** . . . . נָתַן

no-**tayn** . . . . . . נֹתֵן, נוֹתֵן

na-**ta**-ta . . . . נָתַתָּ

ס

sav-**ray** ma-ra-**nan**. סָבְרֵי מָרָנָן

see-**door** . . . . סִדּוּר

say-der . . . . סֵדֶר

so-**maych** . . . . סוֹמֵךְ

soo-**ka** . . . . סֻכָּה

soo-**kot** . . . . סֻכּוֹת

se-la . . . . סֶלָה

s-**lach** . . . . סְלַח

s-lee-**chot** . . . . סְלִיחוֹת

say-fer . . . . סֵפֶר

ע

av-d-**cha** . . . . עַבְדְּךָ

av-**de**-cha . . . . עַבְדֶּךָ

ad . . . . עַד

od . . . . עוֹד

o-**zayr** . . . . עוֹזֵר

o-la-**lay**-noo . . . . . עוֹלָלֵינוּ

o-**lam** . . . . עוֹלָם

o-la-**meem** . . עוֹלָמִים, עֹלָמִים

o-**mayd** . . . . עוֹמֵד

o-**say** . . . . . . עוֹשֶׂה, עֹשֶׂה

o-**se** . . . . עוֹשֶׂה, עֹשֶׂה

oz . . . . עֹז, עוֹז

oo-zo . . . . עֻזּוֹ

oo-ze-cha . . . . עֻזֶּךָ

ay-**nay** . . . . עֵינֵי

ay-**ne**-cha . . . . עֵינֶיךָ

ay-**nay**-noo . . . . עֵינֵינוּ

eer . . . . עִיר

al . . . . עַל

ol . . . . עֹל

a-**lai** . . . . עָלַי

a-**lay**-hem . . . . עֲלֵיהֶם

el-**yon** . . . . עֶלְיוֹן

a-**lay**-chem . . . . . . עֲלֵיכֶם

a-**lay**-noo . . . . עָלֵינוּ

ol-**ma**-ya . . . . עָלְמַיָּא

o-la-**meem** . . עֹלָמִים, עוֹלָמִים

am . . . . עַם, עָם

eem . . . . עִם

a-**mo** . . . . עִמּוֹ

a-**meem** . . . . עַמִּים

am-**cha** . . . . עַמְּךָ

a-**me**-cha . . . . עִמָּךְ

ee-**ma**-noo . . . . עִמָּנוּ

o-mer . . . . עֹמֶר

a-**noo** . . . . עֲנוּ

a-**nay**-noo . . . . עֲנֵנוּ

a-**far** . . . . עָפָר

ayts . . . . עֵץ

e-rev . . . . עֶרֶב

a-**sa** . . . . עָשָׂה

o-**say** . . . . . . עֹשֶׂה, עוֹשֶׂה

o-**se** . . . . עֹשֶׂה, עוֹשֶׂה

a-**say** . . . . עֲשֵׂה

a-**see**-ta . . . . עָשִׂיתָ

a-**sa**-noo . . . . עָשָׂנוּ

ayt . . . . עֵת

a-**ta** . . . . עַתָּה, עָתָּה

פ

p-**day** . . . . פְּדֵה

poo-**reem** . . . . פּוּרִים

pee . . . . פִּי

pe-lay . . . . פֶּלֶא

p-**nay** . . . . פְּנֵי

pa-**nav** . . . . פָּנָיו

pa-**ne**-cha . . . . פָּנֶיךָ

pe-sach . . . . פֶּסַח

pa-am . . . . פַּעַם

pa-a-**ma**-yeem . . . . . פַּעֲמַיִם

p-a-**meem** . . . . פְּעָמִים

pree . . . . פְּרִי

צ

tsayt-**chem** . . . . . . צֵאתְכֶם

ts-va-**ot** . . . . צְבָאוֹת

ts-va-**am** . . . . צְבָאָם

Pronunciation	Hebrew
tsa-**deek**	צַדִּיק
tsa-dee-**keem**	צַדִּיקִים
tse-dek	צֶדֶק
ts-da-**ka**	צְדָקָה
tsee-**va**-noo	צִוָּנוּ
tsoor	צוּר
tsoo-**ree**	צוּרִי
tsee-**yon**	צִיּוֹן
tsar	צַר
tsa-**ra**	צָרָה

ק

Pronunciation	Hebrew
ka-**dosh**	קָדוֹשׁ
k-**dosh**	קְדוֹשׁ
k-do-**sheem**	קְדוֹשִׁים, קְדֹשִׁים
ko-desh	קֹדֶשׁ
kod-**sho**	קָדְשׁוֹ
kod-sh-**cha**	קָדְשְׁךָ
kod-**she**-cha	קָדְשֶׁךָ
keed-sha-**noo**	קִדְּשָׁנוּ
kee-**dash**-ta	קִדַּשְׁתָּ
k-doo-shat-**cha**	קְדֻשָּׁתְךָ
k-doo-sha-**te**-cha	קְדֻשָּׁתֶךָ
kol	קוֹל, קֹל
ko-**lay**-noo	קוֹלֵנוּ
koo-**ma**	קוּמָה
ko-**nay**	קוֹנֵה, קֹנֵה
ka-**yam**	קַיָּם
kee-**ma**-noo	קִיְּמָנוּ
ka-**ra**	קָרָא
ka-**rov**	קָרוֹב
ka-**reev**	קָרִיב
ke-ren	קֶרֶן
k-shar-**tam**	קְשַׁרְתֶּם

ר

Pronunciation	Hebrew
ra-**oo**	רָאוּ
rosh	רֹאשׁ
rosh ha-sha-**na**	רֹאשׁ הַשָּׁנָה
ray-**sheet**	רֵאשִׁית
rav	רַב, רָב
ra-**ba**	רַבָּא
ra-**ba**	רַבָּה
ra-**bee**	רַבִּי
ra-**beem**	רַבִּים
reev-**ka**	רִבְקָה
roo-ach	רוּחַ
roo-**chee**	רוּחִי
ro-**fay**	רוֹפֵא, רֹפֵא
ra-**choom**	רַחוּם
ra-**chayl**	רָחֵל
ra-**chaym**	רַחֵם
ra-cha-**me**-cha	רַחֲמֶיךָ
ra-cha-**meem**	רַחֲמִים
ra-cha-**man**	רַחֲמָן
ree-**na**	רִנָּה
ra	רָע
ra-**av**	רָעָב
ra-**a**	רָעָה
ra-ash	רַעַשׁ
ro-**fay**	רֹפֵא, רוֹפֵא
ra-**tsa**	רָצָה
r-**tsay**	רְצֵה
ra-**tson**	רָצוֹן
r-tson-**cha**	רְצוֹנְךָ
r-tso-**ne**-cha	רְצוֹנֶךָ
reesh-**ay**	רִשְׁעֵי
r-sha-**eem**	רְשָׁעִים

ש

Pronunciation	Hebrew
she	שֶׁ
she-a-**dam**	שֶׁאָדָם
she-a-ha-**va**	שֶׁאַהֲבָה
she-a-**hav**-ta	שֶׁאָהַבְתָּ
she-**ayn**	שֶׁאֵין
she-**eem**	שֶׁאִם
she-a-**mar**	שֶׁאָמַר
she-a-**nach**-noo	שֶׁאֲנַחְנוּ
she-a-**nee**	שֶׁאֲנִי
sh-**ar**	שְׁאָר
she-**ba**	שֶׁבָּא
sha-voo-**ot**	שָׁבוּעוֹת
sheeb-**choo**	שִׁבְחוּ
sheev-cha-**cha**	שִׁבְחֲךָ
she-**bayn**	שֶׁבֵּין
sh-vee-**ee**	שְׁבִיעִי
she-b-**chol**	שֶׁבְּכָל
she-ba-sha-**ma**-yeem	שֶׁבַּשָּׁמַיִם
sha-**vat**	שָׁבַת
sha-**bat**	שַׁבָּת
sha-**bat**	שַׁבַּת
she-ha-bo-**ray**	שֶׁהַבּוֹרֵא
she-**hoo**	שֶׁהוּא
she-he-che-**zar**-ta	שֶׁהֶחֱזַרְתָּ
she-he-che-**ya**-noo	שֶׁהֶחֱיָנוּ
she-**hee**	שֶׁהִיא
she-ha-**ya**	שֶׁהָיָה
she-ha-**yoo**	שֶׁהָיוּ
she-ha-**kol**	שֶׁהַכֹּל
she-ha-**me**-lech	שֶׁהַמֶּלֶךְ
she-ha-seem-**cha**	שֶׁהַשִּׂמְחָה
sho-a-**leem**	שׁוֹאֲלִים
sho-**mayr**	שׁוֹמֵר, שֹׁמֵר

sho-**far** . . . שׁוֹפָר
she-cha-**ta**-noo . . . שֶׁחָטָאנוּ
she-ya-**vo** . . . שֶׁיָּבֹא
she-yee-h-**yoo** . . . שֶׁיִּהְיוּ
she-ya-a-**se** . . . שֶׁיַּעֲשֶׂה
sheer . . . שִׁיר
shee-**ra** . . . שִׁירָה
shee-**ra**-ta . . . שִׁירָתָא
she-koo-**lam** . . . שֶׁכֻּלָּם
shel . . . שֶׁל
she-**lo** . . . שֶׁלֹּא
sha-**lom** . . . שָׁלוֹם
sh-lo-**me**-cha . . . שְׁלוֹמֶךָ
she-**lach** . . . שֶׁלָּךְ
shel-**cha** . . . שֶׁלְּךָ
sha-**laym** . . . שָׁלֵם, שַׁלֵּם
sh-**la**-ma . . . שְׁלָמָא
sh-**lay**-ma . . . שְׁלֵמָה
sham . . . שָׁם
shaym . . . שֵׁם
sh-**may** . . . שְׁמֵהּ
sh-**mo** . . . שְׁמוֹ
sh-**mor** . . . שְׁמוֹר, שְׁמֹר
sh-**mai**-ya . . . שְׁמַיָּא
sha-**mai**-yeem . . . שָׁמַיִם, שָׁמָיִם
sheem-**cha** . . . שִׁמְךָ
sh-**me**-cha . . . שְׁמֶךָ
she-mee-**me**-noo . . . שֶׁמִּמֶּנּוּ
sh-**ma** . . . שְׁמַע
she-mak-dee-**sheem** שֶׁמַּקְדִּישִׁים
sho-**mayr** . . . שֹׁמֵר, שׁוֹמֵר
sham-**roo** . . . שָׁמְרוּ
she-ne-e-**mar** . . . שֶׁנֶּאֱמַר
sha-**na** . . . שָׁנָה
shay-**nee** . . . שֵׁנִי
shay-**neet** . . . שֵׁנִית
shee-**nan**-tam . . . שִׁנַּנְתָּם
she-na-**tan** . . . שֶׁנָּתַן
she-na-**ta**-ta . . . שֶׁנָּתַתָּ
sha-**a** . . . שָׁעָה
she-**al** . . . שֶׁעַל
sha-a-**ray** . . . שַׁעֲרֵי
she-a-**sa** . . . שֶׁעָשָׂה
she-a-**see**-ta . . . שֶׁעָשִׂיתָ
she-tsee-**va**-noo . . . שֶׁצִּוָּנוּ
sha-**rayt** . . . שָׁרֵת
she-**sham** . . . שֶׁשָּׁם
shay-shet . . . שֵׁשֶׁת
shtay . . . שְׁתֵּי

שׂ

see-ach . . . שִׂיחַ
seem . . . שִׂים
sam . . . שָׂם
seem-**cha** . . . שִׂמְחָה
seem-**chat** to-**ra** . שִׂמְחַת תּוֹרָה
sa-**ma**-noo . . . שָׂמֵנוּ
s-**fat** . . . שְׂפַת
s-fa-**tai** . . . שְׂפָתַי
sa-**ra** . . . שָׂרָה
sar-**fay** . . . שַׂרְפֵי
s-ra-**feem** . . . שְׂרָפִים
sa-**son** . . . שָׂשׂוֹן

ת

tay-**vayl** . . . תֵּבֵל
t-**hee** . . . תְּהִי
t-**hee**-la . . . תְּהִלָּה
t-hee-**lot** . . . תְּהִלּוֹת, תְּהִלֹּת
t-hee-la-**te**-cha . . . תְּהִלָּתֶךָ
tom-**che**-ha . . . תּוֹמְכֶיהָ
to-**ra** . . . תּוֹרָה
to-**rat** . . . תּוֹרַת
to-ra-**to** . . . תּוֹרָתוֹ
to-rat-**cha** . . . תּוֹרָתְךָ
to-ra-**te**-cha . . . תּוֹרָתֶךָ
t-chee-**la** . . . תְּחִלָּה
tach-**leet** . . . תַּכְלִית
teech-**ra** . . . תִּכְרַע
ta-**meed** . . . תָּמִיד
teem-**loch** . . . תִּמְלוֹךְ
tayn . . . תֵּן
ten . . . תֶּן
teef-**e**-ret . . . תִּפְאֶרֶת
t-fee-**la** . . . תְּפִלָּה
t-fee-**leen** . . . תְּפִילִין
t-fee-la-**tam** . . . תְּפִלָּתָם
teef-**tach** . . . תִּפְתָּח, תִּפְתַּח
t-**kee**-a . . . תְּקִיעָה
toosh-b-**cha**-ta . . . תֻּשְׁבְּחָתָא
tee-sha-**va** . . . תִּשָּׁבַע

The Names of God

The Jewish tradition teaches that the name of God must be treated with respect. More traditional Jews will not print the Hebrew name of God except in holy books like the Bible or the prayerbook, nor will they pronounce the Hebrew name of God except in prayer or perhaps in religious study.

This dictionary will list the names of God only in this section. The Hebrew names of God are not included in the general part of the dictionary.

The names of God fall into four categories. We will list each category separately and not in alphabetical order.

---

1. The Most Sacred Name of God

The most singular explicit name of God is the Tetragrammaton, made up of four letters **י** and **ה** and **ו** and **ה**. This combination of letters is never pronounced. It is considered to be the ineffable name of God. If it does appear, it should be read as if it were the name **אֲדוֹנָי** (a-do-**nai**), translated "Lord".

2. Substitutes for The Most Sacred Name of God

These words in category 2 substitute for actually printing the Tetragrammaton. They also refer to the ineffable name of God.

Lord . . . . **יְיָ**
(appears in place of the Tetragrammaton and is pronounced as if it were **אֲדוֹנָי** (a-do-**nai**))

Lord . . . . **יָהּ**
(appears in place of the Tetragrammaton and is pronounced **ya**)

praise the Lord (ha-le-loo-**ya**) **הַלְלוּיָהּ**

CONTINUED ON NEXT PAGE

3. The Name of God as Power

This category is based on the name אֵל **(ayl)**, meaning God as Power. This name of God comes in many forms.

God, God of . . . (**ayl**) אֵל

God . . . (el-lo-**heem**) אֱלוֹהִים

God . . . (e-lo-**a**) אֱלוֹהַּ

God of . . . (e-lo-**hay**) אֱלֹהֵי

and the God of . . . (**vay**-lo-hay) וֵאלֹהֵי

my God . . . (ay-**lee**) אֵלִי

your God . . . (e-lo-**he**-cha) אֱלוֹהֶךָ

your God . . . (e-lo-**ha**-yeech) אֱלוֹהָיִךְ

our God . . . (e-lo-**hay**-noo) אֱלֹהֵנוּ

your God . . . (e-lo-**hay**-chem) אֱלֹהֵיכֶם

God, the God . . . (ha-**el**) הָאֵל

amongst gods . . . (ba-ay-**leem**) בָּאֵלִים

with God . . . (ba-e-lo-**heem**) בָּאֱלֹהִים

like our God . . . (kay-lo-**hay**-noo) כֵּאלֹהֵינוּ

to God . . . (lay-lo-**heem**) לֵאלֹהִים

to our God . . . (lay-lo-**hay**-noo) לֵאלֹהֵינוּ

4. The Name of God by His Attributes

These names of God name him by his attributes. Some of these names are rarely found in the prayerbook.

my Master . . . (a-do-**nai**) אֲדוֹנַי, אֲדֹנָי

our Master . . . (a-do-**nay**-noo) אֲדוֹנֵנוּ

like our Master . . . (ka-do-**nay**-noo) כַּאדוֹנֵינוּ

to our Master . . . (la-do-**nay**-noo) לַאדוֹנֵינוּ

Almighty . . . (sha-**dai**) שַׁדַּי

God's presence . . . (sh-chee-**na**) שְׁכִינָה

the presence of (God) . (sh-chee-**nat**) שְׁכִינַת

his presence . . . (sh-chee-na-**to**) שְׁכִינָתוֹ

the Place . . . (ha-ma-**kom**) הַמָּקוֹם

the Name (referring to God) . (ha-**shaym**) הַשֵּׁם

the Holy One, blessed be He . . . הַקָּדוֹשׁ בָּרוּךְ הוּא (ha-ka-**dosh** ba-**rooch hoo**)

Bibliography

Biblical Translations

The Holy Scriptures According to the Masoretic Text. 2 vols. The Jewish Publication Society of America, Philadelphia, 1955.

Tanakh: A New Translation of the Holy Scriptures According to the Traditional Hebrew Text. The Jewish Publication Society, Philadelphia, 1985.

T'rumath Tzvi: The Pentateuch. Samson Raphael Hirsch, translation and commentary. The Judaica Press, Inc. , New York, 1986.

Prayerbooks

The Authorized Daily Prayer Book, Revised Edition. Joseph H. Hertz. Bloch Publishing Co. , New York, 1975.

Daily Prayer Book, Ha-Siddur Ha-Shalem. Philip Birnbaum. Hebrew Publishing Co. , New York, 1977.

Gates of Prayer: The New Union Prayerbook. Central Conference of American Rabbis, New York, 1975.

Gates of Repentence. Central Conference of American Rabbis, New York, 1978.

Haggadah of Passover. Maurice Samuel. Hebrew Publishing Co. , New York, 1942.

High Holyday Prayer Book. Philip Birnbaum. Hebrew Publishing Co. , New York, 1979.

The Hirsch Siddur. Samson Raphael Hirsch. Philipp Feldheim, Inc. , Jerusalem, 1978.

Mahzor for Rosh Hashanah and Yom Kippur. The Rabbinical Assembly, New York, 1978.

The New Mahzor for Rosh Hashanah and Yom Kippur. Sidney Greenberg and Jonathan D. Levine. Media Judaica, The Prayer Book Press, Bridgeport, CT, 1978.

Sabbath and Festival Prayer Book. The Rabbinical Assembly of America and The United Synagogue of America, USA, 1973.

Siddur Sim Shalom: A Prayerbook for Shabbat, Festivals, and Weekdays. Jules Harlow. The Rabbinical Assembly and The United Synagogue of America, New York, 1985.

The Traditional Prayer Book for Sabbath and Festivals. David De Sola Pool, The Rabbinical Council of America. Behrman House, Inc. , New York, 1960.

The Union Prayerbook for Jewish Worship, Part I. The Central Conference of American Rabbis, New York, 1959.

Dictionaries

Alcalay, Reuben. *The Complete Hebrew-English Dictionary, Revised Edition.* Media Judaica, Inc. and The Prayer Book Press/Hartmore House, Bridgeport, CT, 1974.

The American Heritage Dictionary of the English Language. William Morris, Editor. American Heritage Publishing Co. , Inc. and Houghton Mifflin Co. , New York, 1973.

Brown, Francis, S.R. Driver, and Charles A. Briggs. *A Hebrew and English Lexicon of the Old Testament.* Clarendon Press, Oxford, 1976.

Even-Shoshan, Abraham. *A New Concordance of the Bible.* 4 vols. "Kiryat Sepher" Publishing House Ltd. , Jerusalem, 1977.

Holladay, William L. *A Concise Hebrew and Aramaic Lexicon of the Old Testament.* E.J. Brill, Leiden, The Netherlands, 1988.

Jastrow, Marcus. *A Dictionary of the Targumim, The Talmud Babli and Yerushalmi, and the Midrashic Literature.* 2 vols. The Judaica Press, Inc. , New York, 1975.

Other Books and Materials from EKS Publishing

Teach Yourself to Read Hebrew, 5 cassettes & book

Teach Yourself to Read Hebrew, book only

Prayerbook Hebrew the Easy Way

Prayerbook Hebrew Teacher's Guide

The First Hebrew Primer

Primer Answer Book

Primer Teacher's Guide

Primer Flashcards

Hebrew Alphabet Chart Set

Handy Hebrew Alphabet

Handy Hebrew Verb Charts

Hebrew Grammar Poster Set

Handy Hebrew Grammar Charts

Top 100 Hebrew Flashwords

Sounds of Hebrew Bingo

Sounds of Hebrew Flashcards

Our Goals

EKS Publishing Company is committed to making the basic sources of Judaism accessible to everyone. Whether your goal is to follow the services, understand the prayerbook, or read the Bible in its original form, our publications offer something to help you. Through our selection of textbooks, dictionary, study aids, and games, we have done our best to demystify classical Hebrew.

THIS IS THE END OF THE BOOK